RACISM IN AMERICAN PUBLIC LIFE

THE MALCOLM LESTER PHI BETA KAPPA
LECTURES ON LIBERAL ARTS AND
PUBLIC LIFE

DAVID A. DAVIS, EDITOR

RACISM IN AMERICAN PUBLIC LIFE

A Call to Action

JOHNNETTA BETSCH COLE

UNIVERSITY OF VIRGINIA PRESS

Charlottesville and London

University of Virginia Press
© 2021 by the Rector and Visitors of the University of Virginia
All rights reserved
Printed in the United States of America on acid-free paper

First published 2021

9 8 7 6 5 4 3 2 1

Library of Congress Cataloging-in-Publication Data

Names: Cole, Johnnetta B., author.
Title: Racism in American public life : a call to action / Johnnetta
    Betsch Cole.
Description: Charlottesville : University of Virginia Press, 2021. |
    Includes bibliographical references.
Identifiers: LCCN 2020024759 (print) | LCCN 2020024760 (ebook) |
    ISBN 9780813945620 (hardcover) | ISBN 9780813945637 (epub)
Subjects: LCSH: Racism in higher education—United States. |
    African Americans—Education (Higher)—Social aspects. |
    Educational equalization—United States. | United States—Race
    relations.
Classification: LCC LC212.42 .C65 2021 (print) | LCC LC212.42
    (ebook) | DDC 379.2/60973—dc23
LC record available at https://lccn.loc.gov/2020024759
LC ebook record available at https://lccn.loc.gov/2020024760

Cover art: Elements from Shutterstock (Artush, andersphoto, Kues,
kpboonjit, photka). Hand lettering by Derek Thornton, Notch Design.

*This book is dedicated to my brother, John Thomas Betsch, Jr.,
whose love of books, art, and music speaks to the power and
beauty of a liberal arts education.*

CONTENTS

FOREWORD

Mercer University in Macon, Georgia, hosts the Malcolm Lester Phi Beta Kappa Lectures on the Liberal Arts and Public Life each year as part of our Phi Beta Kappa induction ceremony. The lectures allow our students to meet an important figure in American higher education and to have conversations about the value of a liberal arts education. This experience reinforces the significance of each student's accomplishment in being inducted into Phi Beta Kappa, and the conversations can be inspiring, but a series of lectures and conversations among a small group of people has a limited effect. Dr. Malcolm Lester had a vision for a series of lectures that supports the mission of the Phi Beta Kappa Society and that reaches a broad audience to influence the discourse about liberal arts in the United States.

Dr. Malcolm Lester, a 1945 graduate of Mercer, returned to the university after graduate school at the University of Virginia to teach history and was named dean of the College of Liberal Arts and Sciences in 1955. In 1959, he left Mercer to join the faculty of Davidson College, where he taught for the next thirty years. While at Davidson, he served as a Phi Beta Kappa senator and member of the Committee on Qualifications, which reviews schools' applications to shelter chapters of the Phi Beta Kappa Society. He felt strongly that Mercer should also shelter a chapter, and he encouraged faculty to apply. In 2007, he made a gift for a lecture series on the liberal arts at Mercer to commence once the university sheltered a chapter of the Phi Beta Kappa Society. Mercer received a charter in 2016. Dr. Lester's bequest states that "the income of such endowed fund shall be used to pay for the delivery of and publication of an annual oration to be delivered by a distinguished scholar at the annual initiation of members in course of Phi Beta Kappa." The lectures are published by the University of Virginia Press, as requested by Dr. Lester, who was inducted into Phi Beta Kappa as a graduate student at the university.

The lecture series focuses on the relationship between the liberal arts and public life. This relationship has been a contentious issue in the recent past. Many politicians have publicly disparaged liberal arts majors, including President Barack Obama, who once dismissed the value of studying art history, and Senator Marco Rubio, who claimed that we need fewer philosophers. The most common criticism is that liberal arts degrees are of less economic value than vocational or professional programs. In the years following the Great Recession, most states significantly cut appropriations for higher education, and funding in many states is still below 2008 levels. Meanwhile, enrollment in many liberal arts programs has declined since 2008. A 2018 study from the American Enterprise Institute found that the number of undergraduates earning bachelor's degrees in some liberal arts subjects, such as English, history and philosophy, fell by at least 15 percent between 2008 and 2016, even though the total number of bachelor's degrees awarded rose 31 percent during that period. The data shows that students are gravitating to applied sciences, engineering, and business, and many of them are following the conventional wisdom that these programs lead more predictably to careers with secure incomes.

The fallout from this shift has had serious consequences for higher education. Some schools have eliminated liberal arts programs with declining enrollment. Several schools have eliminated majors in philosophy and foreign languages, and others have cut or reduced core disciplines such as history and English or relegated humanities and social sciences programs to service components supporting programs that are more vocational in nature. An even greater concern is the fact that dozens of small colleges specializing in liberal arts have closed or consolidated since 2008 due to low enrollment and declining revenue. Under the circumstances, it is unsurprising to see think pieces in major publications proclaiming the end of the liberal arts.

This situation requires us to think about the relationship between the liberal arts and public life. We must ask if the liberal arts serve a useful or necessary purpose, if they are economically valuable, and if we should consider moving to different academic paradigms. Despite the current trends, numerous studies indicate that the liberal arts have considerable practical value. A 2014 study from the American Association of Colleges and Universities, for example, found that 93 percent of employers agree that job candidates' demonstrated capacity to think critically, communicate clearly, and solve complex problems is more important than their undergraduate major. The contemporary workplace is a highly dynamic environment, and it requires and rewards skills that make people adaptable, creative, and collaborative, which are precisely the skills that a liberal arts education develops.

A study by the Mellon Foundation released in 2019 and titled "The Economic Benefits and Costs of a Liberal Arts Education" found that such an education leads to meaningful economic mobility, which has benefits for individuals in their earning ability as well as numerous positive benefits for society. Contrary to criticism, a liberal arts education makes people employable and productive, and those with liberal arts degrees have lifetime earning potentials comparable to those of people in specialized technical fields. The data, therefore, does not support the movement away from liberal arts in American universities. Instead, it reinforces the value of a liberal arts education for economic development at both the individual and the social level.

Economic impact, however, is a limited means to measure the value of an education, and it does not reflect many of the most important aspects of a liberal arts education, which are abstract yet highly valuable. Rather than being a specific body of content knowledge, education in the liberal arts and sciences is a learning method that teaches students how to find, understand, interpret, and evaluate evidence and information according to scientific, social scientific, and humanistic perspectives. While a large range of academic disciplines are associated with the liberal arts, the crux of the method is interdisciplinary. It is a way of learning that privileges critical thinking, breadth of knowledge, exposure to divergent ideas and perspectives, ethical discernment, civic engagement, rational decision-making, empathy, and lifelong learning. This valuable set of skills empowers a person to be an effective and adaptable worker and to live a free and content life in a civil society. A 2018 study by the American Academy of Arts and Sciences, in fact, found that people with liberal arts educations have high rates of satisfaction with their jobs and with their lives. A liberal arts education has value that benefits a person both quantitatively and qualitatively. Because some of the values are not obvious, however, we need to explain the learning methods to students choosing colleges and academic majors; we need to convince politicians and business leaders that a liberal arts education prepares people for productive careers; and we need to make the argument in public that the liberal arts are beneficial to individuals and society. The Lester Lectures are intended to give key figures in higher education a platform to address these crucial issues.

Dr. Johnnetta B. Cole, president of the National Council of Negro Women, gave the second annual Lester Lectures in April 2019. A powerful and influential advocate for the liberal arts, Dr. Cole has spent her career advocating for diversity and equality in higher education. She studied anthropology at Northwestern University, and as a faculty member at Washington State University and the University of Massachusetts Amherst, she helped to establish the field of African American and Africana studies. She served as president of Spelman College and of Bennett College, and as executive director of the Smithsonian Institution's National Museum of African Art. She has served on the boards of major corporations and charitable organizations and has received numerous honors and accolades, including dozens of honorary doctorates. She was inducted into Phi Beta Kappa by Yale University, and she was a senator in the Phi Beta Kappa Society. The Lester Lectures committee selected Dr. Cole not merely because of her accomplishments, however. We selected her because of her reputation for telling hard truths about higher education.

In her lectures on racism in American public life, Dr. Cole offers a vision for how liberal arts institutions can address racism and be vehicles for change. Many of the components of a liberal arts education—including critical thinking, exposure to different ideas and experiences, and empathy—help to expose the underlying effects of racism on contemporary society. Dr. Cole's lectures look back on her own experiences with racism since her childhood in segregated Jacksonville, Florida, and she explains how racism still affects public life in this country. She recommends that Americans hold what she calls "courageous conversations" to address ongoing racism, and she describes how these honest, interracial conversations can take place productively. She also asserts that institutions of higher education are uniquely capable of hosting these conversations, and that they have both the opportunity and the obligation to address race and racism.

Dr. Tikia K. Hamilton's afterword reflects her experiences attending and teaching at some of the nation's most elite schools, including Princeton University, where she earned a doctorate in history. Using her expanded knowledge of history, she also operates Triple Ivy Writing and Educational Solutions, which provides editorial assistance and content development for writers on various projects, including several with Dr. Cole. Dr. Hamilton gives examples of how liberal arts institutions can promote equality and of the hard truths that we need to share in our courageous conversations. Making higher education accessible and equitable creates the possibility of meaningful racial progress, and using the liberal arts as a vehicle for interracial exchange and understanding can help to ameliorate racism, our country's most enduring social problem.

The Malcolm Lester Lectures provide an important platform for thought leaders to articulate the role of the liberal arts in public life. The Phi Beta Kappa Society is a leading voice advocating for the value and benefits of liberal arts and sciences education, fostering freedom of thought, and recognizing academic excellence. While one specific chapter of the society sponsors the Malcolm Lester Lectures, they reinforce the society's mission to advocate for the liberal arts. Many people likely see the value of the liberal arts as self-evident, but the social and political opposition to liberal arts education indicates that we need to explain how liberal arts and sciences education works, why it matters, and how people benefit from it. The Lester Lectures committee anticipates that this series will continue to offer important contributions to the ongoing discourse about the liberal arts and public life, and we are grateful for our partnership with the University of Virginia Press to make this possible.

DAVID A. DAVIS

RACISM IN AMERICAN PUBLIC LIFE

INTRODUCTION

IT WAS A GREAT honor for me to offer the annual Malcolm Lester Phi Beta Kappa lectures on liberal arts and public life. It was particularly fitting to do so at Mercer University in Macon, Georgia, an institution that is known for its strength in the liberal arts.

Founded in 1833 by a group of Baptists, Mercer is named for its founder and first board chair, Jesse Mercer, a prominent leader in the local Baptist community. In its early years, the school served as an institute for developing manual labor skills among the working classes, prior to becoming more established as a preparatory school. As with many schools during that time, admissions were limited to White boys. African Americans were forced to wait another 130 years before they could be accepted at Mercer.

In 1914, six years before the passage of the Nineteenth Amendment guaranteeing women's suffrage, Mercer Law School admitted Katheryne Carolyn Pierce. She became the first woman to graduate from the law school and the first woman in the state of Georgia to hold a bachelor of law degree. In 1923 Caroline Patterson became the first woman to earn a bachelor of arts degree from Mercer. Patterson was associated with the Daughters of the Confederacy, and she opposed women's suffrage, facts that are reflective of the times in which she lived.

In 1963, in response to two world-historical events—the African independence movement and the civil rights movement—the trustees ended Mercer's exclusionary policies by admitting Sam Oni, a student from Ghana, West Africa. Thus Mercer became one of the few private schools in the South to admit a Black student before the passage of the Civil Rights Act in 1964.

In 1964, Jean Walker came to Mercer as the first African American woman to join the institution in a nonmenial capacity. Walker had turned down her acceptance to Spelman, a historically Black college for women, because she wanted to help integrate Mercer. Despite the ongoing discrimination that she endured on campus, Walker earned a bachelor of science degree in mathematics. After the assassination of Dr. Martin Luther King Jr. on April 4, 1968, she worked with Rev. Ralph Abernathy and the Southern Christian Leadership Conference in organizing the Poor People's Campaign, also called the Poor People's March, in June 1968.

Emerging from its meager beginnings and homogenous roots, Mercer is now in the top tier of national universities in *U.S. News and World Report*'s annual Best Colleges issue. It has grown to serve thousands of students from all walks of life, with an alumni pool that continues to honor the school's mission and that of Dr. Malcolm Lester, who championed the liberal arts over the course of his life and career.

Malcolm Lester was born in 1924 in Georgetown, Georgia, some two hours from Macon. He graduated from Mercer in 1945 at the tail end of World War II, and he went on to earn a master of arts degree and a doctorate in philosophy from the University of Virginia. While attending UVA, Lester was inducted into the Phi Beta Kappa Society.

A notable historian and a Fulbright scholar, Dr. Lester was a professor and dean of Mercer's College of Liberal Arts and Sciences and also taught at Davidson College in North Carolina during a career that ultimately spanned more than thirty years. He was deeply invested in sustaining the liberal arts at Mercer and beyond, and it was he who endowed the Phi Beta Kappa lectures on the liberal arts and public life. Dr. Lester understood the critical role that the liberal arts play in the education of citizens in a democratic society. And he believed, as I do, that critical thinking and learning across a broad array of subjects can help prepare students to adapt more readily to diverse work environments. Dr. Lester also believed, as I do, that a liberal arts education can help instill in students a sense of civic obligation.

In these critical times, we cannot overestimate the value of a liberal arts education. Nor can we overestimate the need for civic engagement, which Mercer University fosters through its many undergraduate and graduate offerings.

"A liberal arts degree is more important than ever," observed former Amherst dean and education columnist Willard Dix in a 2016 article by that title in the business-centric magazine *Forbes*. "It encourages the questioning of assumptions and reliance on facts as well as an understanding that even facts can be interpreted differently through different lenses." Such critical inquiry is vitally important in this era of "fake news," where it is often difficult to determine which news items are credible and which are being generated by individuals who have a sinister agenda.

The late Steve Jobs, co-founder of Apple Inc. and a giant in the field of technology, also attested to the significance of the liberal arts in an age of evolving science and rapid innovation. He said: "It is in Apple's DNA that technology alone is not enough—it's technology married with liberal arts, married with the humanities, that yields us the results that make our heart sing—and nowhere is that more true than in these post-PC devices."[1]

In recent years, liberal arts programs have come under attack. The state of Wisconsin is a striking example of where this is happening. As reported in an article in the *Atlantic,* Wisconsin was once regarded as the home of one of the finest public university systems in the nation. Much of this stemmed from the "Wisconsin Idea," a concept promoted by University of Wisconsin president Charles Van Hise, who championed the idea that learning should transcend campus experiences. Additionally, Van Hise said, "the search for truth" should endure as a lifelong process and serve as the foundation upon which people engage in various careers, professions, and leadership roles. "I shall never be content until the beneficent influence of the University reaches every family of the state," Van Hise wrote in 1905, reflecting what he regarded as the ultimate mission of the state university system.

In 2015, Wisconsin governor Scott Walker released an administrative budget proposal that challenged Van Hise's outlook while opting for a bottom-line approach to public education that emphasized market needs, most especially the high-tech economy. Walker's proposal met with considerable backlash, such that he backed down from his push against the liberal arts. Nevertheless, one of the University of Wisconsin's affiliate schools at Stevens Point subsequently announced plans to scrap thirteen liberal arts majors, including history. Fortunately, Wisconsin residents voted against the changes, electing Tony Evers, a governor who appears more invested in sustaining and promoting the liberal arts. However, Evers still faces challenges from the state legislature.[2]

There are many ways to describe the value of a liberal arts education. However, I think certain attributes have particular value at this particular time in American public life. A liberal arts education prepares students to adapt and thrive in an ever-changing world; to see things from different perspectives; to be comfortable with different cultures and ideas; to engage in learning throughout their lives; and to enjoy lives that are rich with meaning and purpose.

Unfortunately, since the founding of our great nation, distorted notions about race and the practice of racism have stood in opposition to the ideals of a liberal arts education.

My three Malcolm Lester Phi Beta Kappa lectures, which have been expanded into the three chapters of this book, focused on race and racism in American public life. In the first chapter, "Race and Racism in American Public Life: Lessons from My Life and from Anthropology," I invite reflection on the various ways that the pernicious practice of racism—including the belief that African Americans are inferior to White Americans—continues. In addition to drawing on lessons from my own life, I reflect on how we might use insights from the field of anthropology to challenge racist thinking and provide solutions to racist behaviors.

The second chapter is entitled "The Need for Courageous Conversations about Race and Racism in American Public Life." With full appreciation of how difficult it is to do so, I issue a call for serious dialogue about the racist practices that continue to haunt Americans and that keep us from making progress toward a more perfect union. At the conclusion of the chapter, I offer suggestions for how Black and White Americans might engage in these conversations.

The third chapter is entitled "Imagine Our Nation without Racism: A Call for Action in the Academy." After reviewing the history of race and racism in American higher education, I suggest specific steps we can and must take to bring greater diversity, equity, accessibility, and inclusion into the American academy.

As I was completing my final revisions for this book, two monumental events occurred in the United States. The first was the outbreak of the COVID-19 pandemic, the most deadly health crisis since the flu pandemic of 1918. The second was the police killing of George Floyd in Minneapolis on May 25, 2020, and the subsequent demonstrations that in June alone involved as many as 26 million people nationwide, with more than 40 percent of U.S. counties participating in the protests.[3]

The two pandemics are connected in the sense that the coronavirus outbreak has exposed the systemic racial and economic inequality that continues to afflict our nation. I refer to both the current health crisis and this period of racial turmoil as pandemics because each has spread across our nation and our world.

As I write this addendum in late July 2020, the novel coronavirus has infected almost 18 million people worldwide and resulted in more than 650,000 deaths. Our nation has been disproportionately affected. While the United States makes up less than 5 percent of the world's population, we currently account for more than one-quarter of all COVID-19 cases and almost a quarter of deaths. There have been more than 4.5 million reported cases, and more than 150,000 Americans have lost their lives to the disease.[4]

The novel coronavirus has been called a great equalizer because it has impacted every person in our country in some way. However, the description is not accurate, because traditionally marginalized communities have been impacted far more than other populations. African Americans, Latinxs, Native Americans, the poor, and other marginalized communities have experienced significantly higher infection, hospitalization, and death rates from COVID-19 than White Americans. Indeed, hospitalization rates for African Americans and Native Americans are five times greater than those for White Americans, and rates for Latinxs are four times greater.[5]

These numbers illustrate how unequal access to quality health care, housing, and employment has deleterious effects on marginalized communities. Health officials repeatedly urge people to practice social distancing, to wear masks, and to wash their hands often. These guidelines assume that everyone has access to what is needed to practice good public health. That is not the case. For example, many homes on rural Native American reservations and in Alaskan Native villages do not have adequate sanitation, including access to clean running water. In May 2020 the Navajo Nation had the third highest per capita rate of COVID-19, surpassing New Jersey and New York.[6]

In addition, communities of color and other traditionally marginalized groups are often caught in a vicious cycle that creates increased chances of exposure to the coronavirus. Many people can obey the orders to stay away from public places, to work from home, and to avoid close contact with other people. However, a large number of individuals in marginalized communities cannot afford to do so. Many Black and Latinx people of color cannot shelter at home because they work in "essential" job sectors such as transportation, the restaurant industry, public safety, hospitals, and grocery stores that bring them into contact with large groups of people.[7]

The virus also disproportionately affects the children of traditionally marginalized groups. As schools transitioned to remote, online learning in order to practice social distancing, these children faced barriers that those in more affluent school districts were not subjected to. Disparities in broadband adoption, commonly called the digital divide, stem from systemic racism and income inequality. Nearly half of all people in the United States without internet access at home are people of color. Approximately 15 million children in our country (21 percent of all children) live in families with incomes below the federal poverty threshold. And the percentage of Black children in poverty is at least twice as high as among White children.

These children often live in conditions and family situations that are far from ideal for distance learning. How does a child effectively participate in remote learning when there is only one computer in a home? How does a child concentrate on homework when there is no designated quiet place to do so?[8]

In another illustration of how the coronavirus has disproportionately affected a particular community, hate incidents directed at Asian Americans and Pacific Islanders have sharply increased, driven at least in part by the use of the terms "Chinese virus" and "Kung Flu" by President Donald Trump. Organizers and supporters of the group Stop AAPI Hate documented 832 incidents across California from April through June 2020. Among them were 81 incidents of assault and 64 potential civil rights violations.[9]

The second pandemic, that of racial turmoil, was triggered or at least abetted by a string of violent acts by the police and others against people of color.

The names George Floyd, Rayshard Brooks, and Tony McDade are just the latest to be indelibly connected to police violence—joining those of Eric Garner, Walter Scott, Michael Brown, Freddie Gray, Philando Castile, and others. And the shooting of Ahmaud Arbery by two civilians shows how "jogging while Black" and similar innocuous activities can lead to death.

The killing of unarmed Black women does not receive the same degree of attention as the killing of unarmed Black men. This is a reflection, in my view, of the ongoing presence of what Frances Beal called double jeopardy in a pamphlet of that title that she wrote in 1969. Indeed, Black women can be victimized twice—because of their race and because of their gender.[10]

So we must call the names of unarmed murdered Black women just as we call those of unarmed murdered Black men: Breonna Taylor, Aiyana Stanley-Jones, Tanisha Anderson, Atatiana Jefferson, Charleena Lyles, and so many others.

The protests that began in May 2020 in response to the deaths of unarmed Black women and men are organized mainly by the Black Lives Matter (BLM) movement. Using the hashtag #BlackLivesMatter on social media, the movement was founded in 2013 by three young Black women—Alicia

Garza, Patrisse Khan-Cullors, and Opal Tometi—after the acquittal of George Zimmerman in the February 2012 shooting death of Trayvon Martin, an African American teen. After the 2014 deaths of Michael Brown and Eric Gardner, the movement became nationally known for its anti-racist advocacy and protest. Today it's a global organization that also is active in the United Kingdom and Canada.

In this country, BLM is a decentralized network with more than thirty chapters. The movement is also connected to other organizations that share its mission. While Black Lives Matter protests have been centered in the U.S., similar protests over improper police treatment of people in communities of color have occurred around the world.[11]

What is it about the death of George Floyd that triggered such a strong and sustained reaction to police violence and systemic racism at this particular time in American history? I believe there are two factors. The first is how Floyd was killed by an officer who pressed his knee on his neck for almost nine minutes. The image of this brutal act, while two police officers stood by and watched as Floyd struggled to breathe, called up for me and for countless other African Americans images of shackles around the necks of enslaved Black people.

In his powerful eulogy delivered at Floyd's funeral, Rev. Al Sharpton drew on this collective memory. Rev. Sharpton passionately stated what many African Americans feel deep down in their souls: "George Floyd's story has been the story of Black folks. Because ever since 401 years ago, the reason we could never be who we wanted and dreamed to be is you kept your knee on our neck. . . . It's time for us to stand up in George's name and say, 'Get your knee off our necks!'"[12]

The murder of George Floyd conjures up another image that is associated with the necks of Black people—that of racial violence in the form of lynching. Although Whites, Latinxs, Native Americans, and Asian Americans have also been lynched in the U.S., the vast majority of the victims of this profoundly brutal form of murder have been Black people—specifically Black men, although Black women and children have also been subjected to this barbaric act.

Lynching historically has been a form of racial terrorism to perpetuate White supremacy and the oppression of Black people. There have been close to 4,500 documented cases of the lynching of Black men, women, and children in the United States.[13]

The second factor that triggered the mass protests that began in May 2020 is the novel coronavirus pandemic itself, which put the majority of Americans under stay-at-home orders for at least several months. Millions of people confined to their homes spent more than the usual amount of time watching TV news broadcasts and reading information on social media platforms. The murder of George Floyd and other acts of police violence were caught on smartphones and brought into living rooms via the media. As the images were played over and over again, commentators recalled the infamous and brutal police beating of Rodney King in Los Angeles in 1991. After thirty years was there still no end to such violence? The outcry began: "Enough is enough!"

I should note that while I condemn the killing of unarmed women and men by police, I have a personal reason for urging that we not label all police departments and all police officers as racist and violent. One of my sons is a sergeant in a police department. In conversations with him, I have come to understand how difficult, dangerous, and often thankless his job is.

Whatever the mixture of factors that produced these intense and sustained protests, our country seems to be in a different place than it was just a few months ago. And I am very cautiously optimistic that this time we might see meaningful change in addressing systemic racism.

As someone who has long struggled against racism, sexism, and other systems of inequality, I welcome the incredible diversity among the protestors. I am especially impressed by the number of young White people marching and calling for an end to systemic racism.

It is encouraging to hear that some police chiefs and officers are supporting change in their organizations. And there is hope that Congress might pass legislation backing needed changes, such as the outlawing of chokeholds and the establishment of a nationwide database of law enforcement officers.

I am also encouraged by the number of companies, sports leagues, organizations, politicians, and individuals who are acknowledging systemic racism and inequality in the United States. Indeed, players, coaches, and owners of all major U.S. professional sports leagues—Major League Baseball, the National Basketball Association, the Women's National Basketball Association, the National Hockey League, and the National Football League—as well as drivers and others involved with the National Association for Stock Car Auto Racing (NASCAR) have made statements and taken actions in support of the Black Lives Matter movement.

There have even been statements supporting the movement from several professional European soccer leagues, where racism also remains an issue.

I am most struck by the responses to the recent protests from the NFL and NASCAR. Not only were these actions poignant and powerful, both showed how one individual or a small number of people can bring about positive change. In the words of the cultural anthropologist Margaret Mead: "Never doubt that a small group of thoughtful, committed citizens can change the world; indeed, it's the only thing that ever has."

The NFL's official change in its position towards the BLM movement is noteworthy. In 2016, after Colin Kaepernick began taking a knee during the playing of the national anthem to protest the treatment of African Americans and other marginalized communities in the U.S., the league office and the majority of owners were not only reticent to address systemic racism, they used the power of their positions to discourage players from peacefully protesting and speaking out in support of the movement.

Amid the ongoing protests in the wake of the killing of George Floyd, Bryndon Minter, a White social media employee of the NFL, decided to take action. On his own, without league approval, Minter asked prominent players to record a video calling on the league to condemn racism and police brutality and to support African American NFL players and the BLM movement. The powerful video, titled "Stronger Together," prompted NFL commissioner Roger Goodell to record a response in which he apologized for not supporting the African American players and stated that the league supports peaceful protests against systemic racism.[14]

In another example, Daniel Snyder, majority owner of the NFL's Washington Redskins, had long resisted calls to remove the derogatory term from the team's name. He has finally agreed to review a change. Following his decision, the Cleveland Indians announced that they also will review the name of their team.

Recent events surrounding NASCAR, the most conservative of the major professional sports in the U.S., illustrate a change in how participants and owners acknowledge the history of a significant racial divide between the North and the South. NASCAR has a strong following in the South, and the vast majority of its fans are White. Bubba Wallace, the only African American driver, urged NASCAR to ban the Confederate flag at its events as a statement that the sport wishes to be inclusive of diverse fans. In June 2020, NASCAR did just that.[15]

Companies across our country, from small businesses to Fortune 500 multinationals, have come out in support of BLM and the call to acknowledge systemic racism and promote policies that encourage diversity and inclusion in workplaces. Blue-chip corporations such as Walmart, Home Depot, Apple, Amazon, Microsoft, McDonald's, Uber, and many more have issued statements supporting BLM and have pledged more than $500 million to date to fight racial inequality.[16] Companies whose products are associated with racist stereotypes have announced that advertising images for Aunt Jemima pancake mix and syrup, Uncle Ben's rice, Eskimo Pies, and Land O'Lakes butter will be changed.[17]

The military has begun discussions to remove the names of Confederate soldiers from its bases. And Mississippi, the last state with a flag displaying the Confederate battle emblem, has voted to redesign it.

Two major foundations that support the arts and culture are committed to funding work that advances social justice. At the Ford Foundation, this has been the focus since Darren Walker assumed the presidency in 2013.

The Andrew W. Mellon Foundation, the largest funder of the arts and humanities in the United States, recently announced the reorientation of its grant-making program through the lens of social justice. Under the leadership of president Elizabeth Alexander—poet, essayist, playwright, professor, and former director of the Ford Foundation's Creativity and Free Expression program—the foundation will now evaluate all applications based on one principal question: Will this proposal help create a more just and fair society? Although the change has been in the works since Alexander became president two years ago, she noted that current events have made the shift in priorities all the more essential.

Schools, colleges, and universities are renaming buildings and programs that bear the names of individuals who are closely associated with racism. For example, Princeton University removed Woodrow Wilson's name from its prestigious School of Public and International Affairs.[18] Across the nation, academic institutions, towns, cities, and states are removing statues that honor historical figures who either promoted or were clearly associated with enslavement and systemic racism. A number of such statues have also been torn down by protestors.

We have reached a moment of change in our country that I hope can be sustained. However, we have been at similar hopeful moments in the past that did not last. In addition, our momentum is threatened by the "law and order" backlash in response to efforts to address systemic racism in all sectors of American society.

These two movements—the call to address systemic racism, and the call to defend what are said to be "American values"— are gaining even more attention as our country heads into the 2020 presidential elections.

Regardless of one's party affiliation, it should be clear that President Trump and his loyal Republican supporters firmly oppose the Black Lives Matter movement as they speak and act in terms of a cultural war. For example, in the middle of a substantial increase in the number of COVID-19 cases, the president held an event on July 3 at Mount Rushmore—despite protests by Native Americans that the land is sacred to them, and despite the concerns of public health officials about the gathering of 7,500 supporters who did not practice social distancing and who were not required to wear masks.

At the event, Trump spoke of "a merciless campaign to wipe out our history, defame our heroes, erase our values, and indoctrinate our children." And, he referred to those protesting the killing of George Floyd and other Black Americans as "angry mobs [who] are trying to tear down statues of our founders, deface our most sacred memorials, and unleash a wave of violent crime in our cities." He added: "In our schools, our newsrooms, even our corporate boardrooms, there is a new far-left fascism that demands absolute allegiance."[19]

As the issues that are dividing Americans in our current state of racial turmoil become more and more intense, the three Phi Beta Kappa Mercer lectures that I presented in 2019, and that are the basis of this book, have new importance.

In them, I lifted up the critical importance of the humanities in the kind of effective education that is needed in our schools, colleges, and universities. I also encouraged the teaching of the history of racism in our country as a prerequisite to combating it. And I called for courageous conversations about race and racism to take place in the academy as well as in our communities.

It is my hope that everyone who reads this book will find something that is helpful in their ongoing efforts to understand and challenge racism in American public life. As expressed in this paraphrase capturing what Dr. Martin Luther King Jr. said during his March 1965 sermon in Selma, Alabama: Our lives begin to end the day we become silent about things that matter.[20]

1

RACE AND RACISM IN AMERICAN PUBLIC LIFE

Lessons from My Life and from Anthropology

Education is the most powerful weapon which you
can use to change the world.

—*Nelson Mandela*

AS I GREW UP in Jacksonville, Florida, during the days of legal segregation, the awareness of race was an ever-present reality in my life. Deeply etched into the practices of most White southerners was the belief that all Black people were inferior to all White people. These beliefs were often the byproducts of "scientific racism."

Throughout its long history, scientific racism attempted to give credence to the belief that some races are superior to others. While there was never anything scientific about this brand of racism, it became the mainstay of some of the world's leading philosophers. In the eighteenth and early nineteenth centuries, English physician Charles White suggested that races were distinct from one another via "The Great Chain of Being," a hierarchy ordained by God. During this same time, Benjamin Rush, a signer of the Declaration of Independence and a leader in the American Enlightenment, positioned Blackness as a hereditary disease. Future U.S. president Thomas Jefferson, a scientist, politician, and slaveholder, opined at length about racial theory in his *Notes on the State of Virginia*, arguing that African Americans, and to a lesser extent Native Americans, were less intelligent than White people, less endowed with the gifts of beauty and foresight, and more prone to caprice and impulsiveness.

These notions about race may sound strange today. But it is important to remember that they formed the basis of the writings of many scholars, including the much-revered Friedrich Hegel and Immanuel Kant. The theories of scientific racism were common until World War I, when many theories of racial difference became discredited. However, the notion of racial differences in intelligence was certainly being promoted in 1994 in the popular text *The Bell Curve*, by Richard J. Herrnstein and Charles Murray.

Theories of racial difference also undergirded the so-called "separate but equal" laws that codified racist beliefs in the South. Under slavery, African Americans frequently lived and worked in close proximity to those who regarded them as mere property. However, once slavery ended, the majority of White people insisted that wherever possible the two races should remain apart. Such thinking enjoyed legal sanction when in 1896 the Supreme Court ruled in *Plessy v. Ferguson* that segregation was constitutionally sound. Thereafter, states began to adopt

Jim Crow laws and practices that provided for segregated education, accommodations, recreation, and travel. In some places, Mexican Americans and Asian Americans were subjected to similar laws and practices. However, at times, theories about racial differences positioned Mexican Americans and Asian Americans closer to the White end of a continuum, far away from Black people. Added to the widespread disenfranchisement of Black people in the South, all of these practices had the effect of reinforcing stereotypes. As Black Americans became relegated to poorer and under-resourced neighborhoods and schools, they became more readily stamped with the badge of inferiority. Historically, and today, Black Americans are associated with high rates of crime, disease, and all that is bad, while White people are more closely associated with progress, cleanliness, and all that is good.

As a child in Jacksonville in the 1940s and '50s, I lived in an all-Black neighborhood and attended all-Black schools. In public places, I was forced to drink from "colored" water fountains, and I ate at similarly designated lunch counters. I could occupy seats only in the back of the bus. When traveling by train, I was forced to ride in cars reserved for "colored" people. A sign in a Jacksonville park said, "No Negroes, Jews, or dogs allowed." That was life under Jim Crow.

When White children received new schoolbooks, my school for "colored children" was given their old ones. The textbooks were filled with the stories of White people who were called heroes and heroines, such as Christopher Columbus, George Washington, Thomas Jefferson, Susan B. Anthony, and Elizabeth Cady Stanton. Years later, I wondered why women and men were being revered when they had promoted racist ideas and practices.

However, my parents, family, teachers, and civic and religious leaders taught me a radically different message about race than the one that was promulgated in racist narratives. There is no such thing as a superior or inferior race, they insisted. Indeed, they drilled into me the belief that my potential was as great as that of any White youngster. Even as a child, my intuition led me to believe that I was not fundamentally different from people who possessed less melanin in their skin than I did.

My religious upbringing, which included attending a Black church, helped to reinforce this belief. Black churches have long been a voice for liberation. In Sunday school I was taught to sing "Red and yellow, Black and White, they are precious in His sight, for He loves the little children of the world." And I remember my teacher explaining that this song meant that although God created people in different colors, they were all equal in His eyes.

In the early years of my education in segregated schools, I learned that Black people had made great contributions to our nation and our world. Stories of heroes and sheroes like Crispus Attucks, Sojourner Truth, Harriet Tubman, and George Washington Carver were lifted up in my classrooms throughout the year, not just during Black History Week—which much later became Black History Month. These heroes and sheroes continued to inspire me as I became active in the civil rights movement of the 1950s and '60s.

As a youngster, I was especially fortunate to know Dr. Mary McLeod Bethune, a shero we read about in my segregated school who became one of the most important Black educators and civil and women's rights leaders in the United States. Born in Mayesville, South Carolina, in 1875, she was one of seventeen children of parents who had been enslaved. Mary Jane McLeod walked five miles to and from a segregated school where she fell in love with the power of education. Years later, as Dr. Bethune, she founded the school that is today Bethune-Cookman University. She served as the only woman in President Franklin Roosevelt's "Black Cabinet;" she was a co-founder of the United Negro College Fund; and in 1935 she founded the National Council of Negro Women, the organization I have the extraordinary privilege of serving as chair of the board and seventh president.

Dr. Bethune and my great-grandfather, Abraham Lincoln Lewis, were close colleagues and friends. A. L. Lewis, as he was known, was Jacksonville's most prominent Black citizen and Florida's first Black millionaire. He had a strong influence on me when I was young. Every Sunday after church, when my sister and I would go to his home for supper, he would ask us the same question: "What are the three 'B' books that will carry you to where you need to go?" We would recite in unison: "The Bible, the schoolbook, and a bankbook." Without minimizing the challenge of being born Black in America, my great-grandfather continued to emphasize that faith, a good education, and financial security would take us a long way.

A. L. Lewis was born in Madison, Florida, in 1865, the year the Civil War ended. Highly influenced by his upbringing in the African Methodist Episcopal Church, he emerged from a position of poverty to become a leading institution-builder and philanthropist.

My great-grandfather was forced to leave school after the sixth grade due to his family's precarious finances. After the family moved to Jacksonville in 1880, he began working as a water boy at a sawmill. He was quickly promoted and became a foreman, a position he held for twenty-two years until he saved enough money to invest in Jacksonville's first Black-owned shoe store.

In 1901, A. L. Lewis joined six other Black men to establish the Afro-American Industrial and Benefit Association, which later became the Afro-American Life Insurance Company, the first insurance company in Florida. Most White-owned insurance companies would not insure Black people, so "the Afro" grew and became profitable.

My great-grandfather's civic engagement was also noteworthy. He helped found the Negro Business League, and he contributed substantially to two historically Black institutions—Edward Waters College and Bethune-Cookman College—and served on their boards of trustees. In 1926 he founded the Lincoln Golf and Country Club, offering African Americans recreational opportunities they were denied at clubs that welcomed only White members.

In 1935, while he was president of the Afro-American Life Insurance Company, A. L. Lewis used funds from the firm's pension bureau to purchase stretches of beachfront property on the Atlantic Ocean forty miles north of Jacksonville. He named the development American Beach. The plan was for the company employees to have a place to vacation, and some would also own homes there. A. L. Lewis said Black people needed and deserved a place where they could enjoy recreation without humiliation. Throughout the 1930s, '40s, and '50s, American Beach was a popular vacation spot for African American people.

As youngsters, my sister and I—and later my brother, who is nine years my junior—would spend most weekends at American Beach. In 2011, American Beach was listed on the National

Register of Historic Places, thanks in large measure to my late sister, MaVynee Osun Betsch, who was known as "the Beach Lady" because of her close association with American Beach.

When I was growing up in Jacksonville, many years before researching one's ancestors became popular, I was told about my maternal lineage, the lineage that connected me to Abraham Lincoln Lewis. Today, dissertations and books are written about my maternal family.

A. L. Lewis married Mary Frances Kingsley Sammis. Mary was the great-granddaughter of Zephaniah Kingsley, a slave owner and trader, and Anta Madjiguene Ndiaye. Anta was born in 1793 into a royal family of the Wolof people, the largest ethnic group in Senegal, West Africa. When she was thirteen she was captured, enslaved, and bought in Havana, Cuba, by Kingsley. Anta Ndiaye became Kingsley's common-law wife, and over time she became manager of his plantation and then a planter and slaveholder as a free Black person in early nineteenth-century Florida. The National Park Service protects and manages the Kingsley Plantation on Fort George Island, where Anta Ndiaye and Zephaniah Kingsley lived. The plantation is a part of the Timucuan Ecological and Historic Preserve.

As the great-granddaughter of the highly respected A. L. Lewis, and as one of three children in an upper-middle-class Black family, I was shielded from some of the racism that other Black youngsters endured on a daily basis. I had access to a good education, which my great-grandfather had been denied but which he nevertheless promoted throughout his life. And because of my family's economic status, I had health care and a full stomach every night, unlike so many Black children of the time—and sadly, unlike many Black children today. However,

I quickly discovered that money could never really protect me from racism. In the final analysis, race always trumped class, especially in the deeply segregated South. And this is as true now as it was then.

Racism is grounded in power and privilege, specifically the power and privilege that come with being White in America. If we hope to ever achieve what Dr. Martin Luther King Jr. described as a "Beloved Community," we must move beyond surface-level discussions about racism that involve simply how people feel about one another and engage in courageous conversations and difficult discussions about power and privilege.

Courageous conversations about race and racism in our country must go back to the period when African people were enslaved and brought in chains to what was to become America. In 1619 the first slave ship arrived in Virginia, then a British colony, carrying between twenty and thirty enslaved Africans. That moment in history set in motion a series of processes and events that would have an enduring impact not only on race relations in the United States, but on how power is unevenly distributed between White Americans and other historically disenfranchised groups.

What a difference it would make if every American would read and examine the 1619 Project—a Pulitzer Prize–winning (and admittedly controversial) interactive initiative guided by *New York Times* journalist Nikole Hannah-Jones that examines the legacy of slavery in the United States—and then engage in discussions about race and racism.[1]

As Jake Silverstein writes in his introduction to the 1619 Project: "Out of slavery—and the anti-Black racism it required—grew nearly everything that has truly made America exceptional: its economic might, its industrial power, its electoral system, its diet and popular music, the inequities of its public health and education, its astonishing penchant for violence, its income inequality, the example it sets for the world as a land of freedom and equality, its slang, its legal system and the endemic racial fears and hatreds that continue to plague it to this day. The seeds of all that were planted long before our official birth date, in 1776, when the men known as our founders formally declared independence from Britain."[2]

Silverstein's words help to underscore the direct relationship between slavery and systems of power. For this reason, in our conversations about race we must include a reckoning of how these systems of power were reified during this same period in places that benefited from slavery even as they sought its abolition. For example, while various states in the North outlawed slavery in the decade or so following the abolition of the transatlantic slave trade, they continued to profit from their investment in the system through the manufacturing of slave-produced products, such as cotton. It is important to point out that although segregation was not legally sanctioned in the North in the post-Emancipation years, the earliest use of the term "Jim Crow" to denote separate accommodations appeared in the *Salem Gazette* of Massachusetts in 1838.[3]

Anti-Black violence was also common in the North, as well as in western states. The attacks on the school that White abolitionist Prudence Crandall established for African American girls in Connecticut during the 1830s stand as a prominent example. Anti-Black violence was also the basis for the New York City draft riots in 1865, when mobs of working-class Whites attacked and killed scores of African Americans, whom they blamed as the principal reason for their being drafted into a war that wealthier Whites could pay to avoid. Additionally, some of the most seemingly resolute White abolitionists in the North held racist beliefs that caused them to consider the mingling of Blacks and Whites as an impossibility, thus leading them to prioritize Black colonization outside of the U.S.

On May 31 and June 1, 1921, mobs of White residents of Tulsa, Oklahoma—many of whom had been deputized and given weapons by city officials—attacked Black homes and businesses in the city's Greenwood district, known as Black Wall Street. What many have called a massacre left between thirty and three hundred people dead, almost all of whom were African American. More than fourteen hundred homes and businesses were burned, and almost ten thousand people were left homeless.

The cause of the race riot was the following: Dick Rowland, a young African American shoeshiner, was accused of assaulting Sarah Page, a White elevator operator. The following day a newspaper reported that Rowland had tried to rape Page and that a lynching was planned for that night.

That evening at the courthouse, where Rowland was being held, a confrontation occurred between an African American man who was trying to protect Rowland and a White protester, leading to the death of the latter. A White mob was incensed, and thus the Tulsa massacre began.

Following the Civil War, African Americans who resided in the North and elsewhere in the country experienced "separate and unequal" access to affordable housing, adequate education, and sustainable employment. Then as now, there was a thin line between *de facto* and *de jure* segregation. Historically, *de jure* describes legal forms of discrimination, such as those sanctioned by *Plessy v. Ferguson,* while *de facto* describes a type of racial discrimination that operates according to custom or seemingly haphazard practices that emerged as the remnants of legally sanctioned discrimination.

As in the South, the type of institutional and structural racism that African Americans faced in the North was made evident by patterns of unequal funding for schooling, especially in the wake of White flight, when opponents of *Brown v. Board of Education* and desegregation fled the cities and carried with them their tax dollars.

The fine line between *de facto* and *de jure* segregation was also reflected in unfair housing patterns, which were supported in great part by government agencies such as the Federal Housing Administration, along with banks and private citizens who refused to loan money, rent, or sell houses to African Americans. In 1948, the Supreme Court ruled against the racially restrictive covenants that White residents used to bar African Americans and other groups from exclusively White neighborhoods. However, this practice continued long after 1948, which helps to explain the White racial homogeneity of suburbs like Levittown, Pennsylvania, beginning in the 1950s.

According to the Equal Justice Initiative, a social justice organization founded by attorney Bryan Stevenson, as late as 1970, sixteen years after *Brown v. Board of Education* and more than twenty years after the Supreme Court ruled against discriminatory housing practices among banks and private citizens, residential segregation in the northern and western parts of the United States was more prevalent than in the South. Indeed, more than four out of five Black residents lived in segregated neighborhoods.

Many of these patterns continue to exist today. The Economic Policy Institute, a nonpartisan think tank, reported that as of 2011, homeownership for Black households stood at nearly 45 percent, compared to around 74 percent for White households. "Since fewer than half of Black households own homes," the report said, "this means that for the median (typical) Black household, there is zero wealth from home equity. The median Black household also owns no stock." And as of 2010, the median net worth for Black families was $4,900, compared to $97,000 for White families.[4]

The Great Recession, which has been described as the most severe economic recession since the Great Depression in the 1930s, occurred just as Barack Obama assumed the presidency of the United States, and it exacerbated existing trends of racial inequality. As economists Heather Boushey and Somin Park wrote in an editorial for the Economic Policy Institute, "Fighting inequality is key to preparing for the next recession." They further stated: "The failure to make a serious dent in high levels of economic inequality in recent years will make responding effectively to the next inevitable recession more difficult, both economically and politically."[5]

However, the impact of the Great Recession was not felt equally by all Americans. An African American saying captures that point: "When White folks have a cold, Black folks have walking pneumonia." While the median wealth of White households sank by nearly 36 percent in the years immediately after the recession, the wealth of Black households plummeted nearly 50 percent, and that of Latinx households was reduced by about 86 percent.

While this book focuses on race and racism, it is important to acknowledge the obvious fact that racism is not the only system of inequality that consistently subjects certain people to bigotry and discrimination. Indeed, millions of Americans suffer from systems of inequality based on gender, gender identity, sexual orientation, religion, class, age, and disability. It is also important to give voice to how life at the intersection of these various identities exacerbates the degree to which individuals are marginalized and oppressed.

Growing up in the segregated South, the prevalence of racism so dominated my everyday life that it was many years before I became fully conscious of the range of ways in which people are discriminated against. It was in the 1980s, when I was a professor at Hunter College, that I was introduced to the theoretical concept and the experienced realities of what Professor Kimberlé Crenshaw calls "intersectionality," a term she coined in 1989.[6]

Intersectionality is an important and useful theoretical framework that can help us understand how various aspects of our social and political identities, such as race, gender, class, and ability, can combine to create specific modes of discrimination. Crenshaw and others have used this theoretical framework to challenge White feminists to consider not only gender but other bases of oppression such as race and class as they negatively impact individuals and institutions.

It was through my collegial relationship and sisterly friendship with Audre Lorde, who was also a professor at Hunter College, that I came to fully grasp the importance of intersectionality. Dramatically, humorously, and effectively, she would illustrate the concept of intersectionality by saying that she did not awaken at 8 in the morning as a Black person who had to hurry and experience what that was like because at 9 she would become a woman for an hour, then at 10 she would become a lesbian, at 11 a mother, at noon a poet . . . and then, as the clock struck 1, she would become a warrior![7] I have heard her say this on more than one occasion. As I read much of what

Audre Lorde wrote, I came to fully understand how and why Black people who are poor and queer do not experience discrimination in the same way as Black people who are middle class and heterosexual.

I also credit Audre Lorde with helping me to understand why it is easier said than done to call for alliances among people who identify most strongly on one basis—for example, race—and those who identify most strongly on another basis—such as gender, religion, sexual orientation, or disability. And not only is the building of alliances easier called for than accomplished, but an individual can be victimized on the basis of one or more identities while victimizing another individual based on another identity.

There is clear evidence that certain groups of people have consistently oppressed other groups. For example, there is a long history of White people oppressing various people of color. However, no group of people is immune to practicing intolerance and discrimination. Today around our world, there are countless examples of groups of people who are subjected to prejudice and victimization but who in turn are prejudiced against and victimize another group of people.

Following the examples of abolitionists turned suffragists like Susan B. Anthony and Elizabeth Cady Stanton and the eugenicist Margaret Sanger, White women can and do experience sexism and simultaneously practice racism. Straight Black people can be intolerant of LGBTQ individuals, as witnessed by the opposition of many religious-minded African Americans to the Marriage Equality Act and their unwillingness to respect and interact with transgender people. Second- and third-generation immigrants can be xenophobic. This is evident in the attitudes of some who support strict and inhumane immigration policies. Jews continue to experience anti-Semitism, as the attacks on synagogues in Pittsburgh and New York in 2018 and 2019 reveal. But Jews can also be islamophobic, for example, promoting stereotypes that characterize all Muslims as terrorists.

When we think of genocide, of course we think of Nazi Germany. But we must remember that in addition to the six million Jews who were killed in and outside of concentration camps during World War II, homosexuals, Gypsies, Catholics, and the mentally ill were also the targets of Nazi hatred based in great part on the theory of eugenics. And how often was it said that a genocide should never happen again . . . and then the world stood by and witnessed the 1990s conflict in Rwanda that made it clear that genocide is not a thing of a long-gone past.

The everyday narrative in the Jim Crow South where I grew up was built on a belief that there are superior and inferior races. Passages in the Bible were often cited to justify why "the Black race" is an inferior race that must forever be subservient to the superior "White race." Today, many years since my college days, I still recall the great sense of vindication I felt in an anthropology class at Oberlin College upon hearing scientific evidence for something I had always thought and believed to be true—that groups of human beings are more alike than they are different from each other.

As I described earlier, scientists and others had set out to prove that certain groups of human beings were not only different from but also inferior to other groups. Whether promoting theories related to social Darwinism or through practices such as ethnographic mapping and even craniology (that is, studying the shape and size of human skulls), individuals inside and outside the academic world perpetuated these theories to advance the notion that the "White race" is superior to "darker races."

James Watson, the renowned Nobel Prize–winning scientist who helped discover the molecular structure of DNA, was stripped of his honorary titles in 2019 for this very reason. During a 2007 interview, Watson had said that he was "inherently gloomy about the prospect of Africa [because] all our social policies are based on the fact that their intelligence is the same as ours—whereas all the testing says not really." Twelve years later, when addressing these comments in a PBS documentary celebrating his scientific achievements, the ninety-year-old Watson insisted that "there's a difference on the average between Blacks and Whites on IQ tests. I would say the difference [is] genetic."[8]

The fact that I am addressing such matters today—not in 1619, when the first documented slave ships arrived on our shores—is a statement about racism as an enduring legacy of slavery. I cannot overstate the importance of acknowledging that the brutality of enslavement, which impacted millions over the course of the transatlantic slave trade, not only in the United States but also in the Caribbean and Latin America, was justified by saying that Black people were inherently inferior to White people. Thus was born the myth of White supremacy that continues to haunt us.

As an anthropologist, I appreciate the importance of understanding the biology of race. However, what is meant by race in everyday parlance is largely socially constructed. In their book *Thinking Race: Social Myths and Biological Realities,* Richard Goldsby and Mary Catherine Bateson present overwhelming evidence that racism results from a misguided combining of biological facts with pernicious socially constructed ideas.[9] Goldsby and Bateson brilliantly help us to understand the reality of human difference and human unity.

The idea that Black and Brown people are more predisposed than White people to criminal behavior is a myth based on the unproven and unprovable notion that there is something in their "racial makeup" that causes these groups to commit more crimes than White people do. The Southern Poverty Law Center refers to "Black-on-White" crime as "the biggest lie in the White supremacist propaganda playbook," noting that "the idea that Black people are wantonly attacking White people in some sort of quiet race war is an untruthful and damaging narrative with a very long history in America."[10] The center offers the savage murder of nine Black parishioners in Charleston, South Carolina, in 2015 at the hands of Dylann Roof as a prime example of how the crime narrative falsely represents Black people as the sole perpetrators of violence and White people as the victims. Roof was quoted as saying, "Y'all are raping our White women. Y'all are taking over the world," as he opened fire on the worshippers. Of course, these claims aren't true, but they are rooted in a history of lynching and the fears of an expanding Black population, which White citizens groups often characterized as "Black invasions" into their communities. The truth is, during the height of Jim Crow, Black folks had much more to fear from the KKK, White lynch mobs, and exclusively White and often racist police departments than vice versa.

President Donald Trump added to the myth of Black criminality when he retweeted false statistics that originated with a neo-Nazi account that inaccurately reported murder rates in Black and White communities. These false claims are also at the center of views about immigrants who have been seeking refuge at our southern border—namely, that they are rapists and criminals who represent what their home countries have to offer. Such falsehoods are also associated with the uneven rates of arrests, convictions, and harsh punishments that African Americans and Latinxs endure relative to their White counterparts, whose blue- and white-collar crimes often fly under the radar of the criminal justice system.

Anthropology, the discipline I was trained in and the lens through which I continue to view the world, can help us better understand key issues and problems in our everyday lives, including racism. As the broadest of all of the disciplines, anthropology examines the vastness of the human experience. Through four subfields—archaeology, biological anthropology, linguistics, and cultural anthropology—anthropology has an enormous amount to say that is meaningful about the biological and cultural diversity and similarities among human beings. And anthropology can certainly teach us a great deal about race and racism in American public life.

Through the study of anthropology, we learn that pitting one group against another occurs in culture after culture and nation after nation. However, we have yet to find a gene that causes this to happen. No matter how widespread and tenacious racism, sexism, and other forms of bigotry are, they are not transmitted genetically. Isn't that good news? What does seem to be genetic is the neurological underpinnings of bias. Our brains, in an effort to protect us, are predisposed to detect differences and make assumptions based on those differences. When we make negative assumptions based on factors such as skin color, gender, and other observable details, we are engaging in bigotry that fuels systems of inequality.

Here is more good news: While the human brain has a limbic system that predisposes us to bias, we also have the largest neocortex of any animal on the planet. That means we have access to more high-order thinking, more conscious awareness than any other animal. And so it is also possible to unlearn discriminatory behaviors and ideas. It is possible to use our inclination towards bias to develop discernment instead of prejudice, to learn how to use wisdom instead of the shorthand of racial stereotypes when faced with someone who differs from us. And the best news is that we could just stop teaching bigotry!

What do wisdom and discernment look like when engaging with the human brain's inclination to detect patterns and differences? If James Watson had used discernment in his interpretation of the gap in IQ scores between Black and White people, he would have come to understand that IQ tests have been shown to predict socioeconomic class better than anything else, including intelligence, potential, or aptitude. This interrogation of the data would have allowed him to see the structures of racism more clearly.

Racism is rooted in the concept and realities of power and privilege. It is the main reason that racists cling so tightly to their worldviews. This was the case during slavery, when many states forbade the acquisition of literacy among enslaved people and sought to limit educational opportunities among free African Americans, who consistently had to thwart attacks on their communities and schools. This was certainly the case with White southerners in the wake of the Civil War and Reconstruction. While they feared social equality and miscegenation (racial mixing), what they feared most of all was the loss of power and privilege that was associated with their white skin. Their attachment to vagrancy laws, chain gangs, and sharecropping, which resulted in inescapable cycles of debt among newly emancipated Black people, illustrates this.

Additionally, the various mechanisms that were devised to strip African Americans of the right to vote—the grandfather clause, poll tax, and literacy test—were rooted in fears that if given the chance, African Americans might excel and prosper in ways that equaled or even exceeded the achievements of White Americans.

The lynching of Black folk, which emerged as an all-too-common phenomenon after slavery, was a means to assure some White people of their power and privilege, and to say to Black people that they had none. According to the Equal Justice Initiative, between 1877 and 1950, White mobs throughout the U.S. hanged, burned alive, shot, drowned, and beat to death some 4,500 African Americans.[11] Of course, these are only the cases that have been documented. Although many lynching victims had been accused of sexually assaulting White women, in most cases the only thing they were guilty of was trying to assert their humanity through actions like exercising the right to vote, engaging in self-defense, owing property or businesses, or daring to share the same sidewalk with White people. The great African American anti-lynching activist and journalist Ida B. Wells-Barnett wrote about this horrific practice as she risked her own life to investigate lynching in the South.

"The alleged menace of universal suffrage having been avoided by the absolute suppression of the Negro vote, the spirit of mob murder should have been satisfied and the butchery of Negroes should have ceased," Wells-Barnett wrote in 1900. She continued: "Negroes were killed for disputing over terms of contracts with their employers. . . . If a colored man resented the imposition of a White man and the two came to blows, the colored man had to die. . . . If he showed a spirit of courageous manhood he was hanged for his pains. . . . In fact, for all kinds of offenses—and, for no offenses . . . men and women are put to death without judge or jury; so that, although the political excuse was no longer necessary, the wholesale murder of human beings went on just the same."[12]

The Equal Justice Initiative data includes documented cases of lynching, but there were many more that we will never know about, such as those that occurred in Texas as a means to control and oppress Mexican people. Despite the various ways that Mexican laborers contributed to the early development of America (on lands that belonged to Mexico prior to White settler colonialism in the nineteenth century and the Mexican-American War), Mexicans and Mexican Americans were often regarded in the same manner as African Americans. Threatened by the prospect of their economic mobility, despite the exploitation of their labor, a racist ideology developed that Mexicans were inferior and should be barred from White establishments and neighborhoods. Horrific forms of violence were committed against Brown people, many of whom were citizens. We know of at least 547 Mexicans and Mexican Americans lynched, including women and children.[13]

While the Equal Justice Initiative records 1950 as the last year that a lynching took place, most of us are aware of the brutal murder of young Emmett Till in 1955, which helped galvanize the civil rights movement. Emmett Till was accused of offending a White woman in her family's grocery store. How he was murdered, while not a lynching by rope, mirrored what happened to other African Americans who were pursued by a mob and subsequently killed because they reportedly defied the mores of a racist society that were designed to keep Black people subservient to White people.

In 1998 in Jasper, Texas—the state where the majority of Mexicans were lynched—three White men murdered forty-nine-year-old James Byrd in what reporters characterized as a "lynching by dragging," demonstrating the extent to which these racist, cowardly acts persisted long past 1950. Byrd had accepted a ride from the men, who were later found to be avowed White supremacists. Instead of taking Byrd home, the men drove him to a remote county road, beat him, urinated and defecated on him, and subsequently chained him by his ankles to the back of their pickup truck. Then they dragged him for approximately three miles. Byrd remained conscious much of the time until his body hit the edge of a culvert, which resulted in the severing of his head and right arm.

The various and recent cases of police brutality against African Americans are examples of the persistence of racism: Amadou Diallo and Sean Bell (New York); Trayvon Martin (Florida); Sandra Bland, Botham Jean, and Atatiana Jefferson (Texas); Philando Castile (Minnesota); Eric Garner (New York); and Oscar Grant (California) are but a few examples that bear this out. And it should be noted that very few of the police officers involved in these cases have been indicted.

Another highly important lesson that anthropology can teach us is the power of human empathy, the ability to identify with another person, to sense what another person is experiencing. Perhaps above all else, human empathy is what will compel us to act on another's behalf. For example, if men really commit to the work of unlearning what Black feminist Patricia Hill Collins frames as the "negative controlling" elements of yet another social construct—gender—they can begin to understand many of the realities in women's lives. The allyship of some men under the #MeToo movement is a testament to this fact, as are efforts among some male legislators to address the gender pay gap.

If we work at it, those of us who are not from Spanish-speaking countries can come to understand the realities of various Latinx communities. And those of us who consider ourselves fully abled can and should engage in the kind of human empathy that would allow us to understand what it is like to be disabled.

Human empathy can help people who are heterosexuals to understand what it is like to suffer from discrimination because one is a lesbian, gay, bisexual, or transgender individual. Through studying history and engaging in serious contemplation, White people have an opportunity to relate to what it is like to be a person of color—Black, Latinx, Native American, or Asian American—in a society that privileges Whiteness. What is required to engage in human empathy is basic and yet far from easy to do—for it is not only to imagine oneself in another's shoes, but to walk in those shoes into multiple experiences of being ignored, belittled, disrespected, violated, and oppressed.

Anthropology is grounded in the notion that no matter how much one reads about the condition of another people, one's understanding will be incomplete without participating in their way of life. This is why anthropologists engage in fieldwork, living among the people they wish to understand. Patterns of segregation and resegregation in our country, including in our schools, often make it difficult for one group of Americans to interact closely with other groups of Americans. Housing costs prevent poor and middle-income people from living near well-to-do people. This means that Black, Brown, and White people often do not live in the same neighborhoods.

Still, it is possible to benefit from cross-cultural experiences in ways that do not reinforce attitudes of superiority that too many have when interacting with different cultures—if we begin from the standpoint of empathy. Thus, whenever we venture beyond our habitual paths to try other people's languages, foods, films, literature, music, and art, we engage in an anthropological process and, more important, come one step closer to bridging the gaps that so often divide us. Some colleges and universities encourage this by urging students to room with people from different backgrounds, participate in a variety of multicultural activities, and study abroad.

The most powerful insight from a cross-cultural experience is that we come to better understand our own culture and ourselves. As the American anthropologist Clyde Kluckhohn said, "It would hardly be fish who discovered the existence of water." Thus a great gift that anyone can receive from experiencing other cultures is insight into one's own way of life.

This brings me to the final lesson that anthropology can help us to understand about race and racism. Change is possible! No matter how stubbornly individuals hold on to ideas and ways that have lost their usefulness or that are destructive to the very fiber of a society, people can change. Furthermore, no matter how deeply racism is etched in a nation's economic, political, religious, and cultural life—in other words, no matter how systemic racism is—that nation can change if the people are willing to do the incredibly difficult work that is required.

It is the will, the determination, the persistence of ordinary and sometimes extraordinary women and men that can transform the world. By her simple but courageous refusal to move to the back of the bus in Montgomery, Alabama, Rosa Parks ignited a movement. The actions of César Chávez and Dolores Huerta, who co-founded the National Farm Workers Association, helped improve the working conditions of countless migrant workers. The efforts of gay activists to make their cause visible after the Stonewall riots in 1969 helped provide the foundation for a concerted movement to establish gay rights in the U.S. The anthropologist Margaret Mead said: "Never doubt that a small group of thoughtful, committed citizens can change the world; indeed, it's the only thing that ever has." And as Dr. Martin Luther King Jr. insisted, we can bring about positive change through education, legislation, and, where necessary, agitation. Of course, he always called for any agitation to be nonviolent.

When I think back to the racist environment in which I grew up and I look out across our country today, I acknowledge that along with the great champions of the civil rights movement, it was the extraordinary efforts and sacrifices of many ordinary people that brought legal segregation to an end.

I want to conclude this chapter by repeating a story that was told by Fannie Lou Hamer. Born in Townsends, Mississippi, in 1917, the last of her parents' twenty children, Ms. Hamer became a voting rights activist, a women's rights activist, a community organizer, and a leader in the civil rights movement. She is also remembered as the co-founder and vice chair of the Freedom Democratic Party. Ms. Hamer would tell this story when she wanted to emphasize who was responsible for doing the work that is required to oppose and hopefully, one day, to eliminate racism.

A group of boys wanted to fool an old lady by asking her a question that they were sure she could not answer. They decided that the ringleader would hold a bird that they had caught behind his back and pose the question: "Old lady, old lady, this bird that I have behind my back, is it dead or alive?" If the old lady said that the bird was dead, he would release his hands and the bird would fly away. But if she said that the bird was alive, he would crush it.

They found the old lady and asked if she would respond to their question. She said she would try. And so the ringleader put the bird behind his back and said: "Old lady, old lady, this bird that I have behind my back, is it dead or is it alive?" With simple but powerful wisdom, the old lady said: "The answer is, it's in your hands!"

Who will do the very difficult work of understanding, opposing, and helping to eliminate racism . . . and all systems of inequality? The answer is: It's in your hands, and it's in mine.

2

THE NEED FOR COURAGEOUS CONVERSATIONS ABOUT RACE AND RACISM IN AMERICAN PUBLIC LIFE

Courage is the most important of all the virtues because without courage, you can't practice any other virtue consistently.

—*Maya Angelou*

"NIGGER, GET OUT OF here!" The little White boy screamed the threat at me from across the street. It was 1941, and I was a five-year-old in Jacksonville, Florida, where I was born and raised. I had accompanied my mother to her appointment at a beauty parlor in the home of one of her friends. Rather than have me stay with her, my mother allowed me to go outside and play.

As I skipped innocently about the neighborhood, I had not a care in the world for the type of social norms that could get a little Black girl killed if she was not careful. Segregation was very real in those days, and Jacksonville's history of racism is as sordid as that of any other place in the Jim Crow South. Unfortunately for me, I had just violated one of Jim Crow's cardinal rules by crossing over into an area designated for Whites only.

"Nigger, get out of here!" The words tore at me as if the boy, no bigger than I was, was attacking me with daggers. In tears, I rushed back to the comfort of a Black neighborhood and my mother's outstretched arms.

Incensed that anyone would treat her child that way, my mother placed aside her righteous indignation to comfort me. That was the first time that I had come face-to-face with racism's diabolical nature. My parents, grandparents, teachers, pastors, and Girl Scout leaders disabused me at a very young age of any notion that I was inherently inferior to White folks, so I knew that a White boy yelling epithets at me was not right. But his words hurt, nonetheless. Even though I was only five, I knew that what had just happened to me was wrong, and I believed such actions should not be allowed—a belief that I have continued to hold throughout my life.

In the three arenas of my professional life—the academy, the world of museums, and as a consultant on issues of diversity, equity, accessibility, and inclusion—I have worked in the interest of social justice, with a special focus on understanding racism and how it intersects with other systems of inequality. During my undergraduate and graduate studies, I was drawn to anthropology, in part because it is a field that addresses race in biological, social, and political contexts.

Over the many years that I worked in the academy, as a professor and then as a college president, I witnessed countless situations that involved injustices based on race. These situations included what was and what was not being taught and learned about different people and their cultures, who the faculty and students were, who held the top leadership positions in American colleges and universities, who did and who did not graduate, and who did what kind of work after they graduated. As I look back over my career in the academy, some of the most difficult but rewarding experiences involved courageous conversations about race and racism in the classroom, in encounters with colleagues, and in settings with guest speakers.

If ever there was a need for such conversations in our country's educational system, it is now, when we hear racist and xenophobic comments from the highest levels of leadership in the United States and around the world. And there should be courageous conversations about racism in our schools, colleges, and universities because such conversations are directly related to what I maintain are the responsibilities of educational institutions. The first responsibility of an educational institution is to help students better understand the world and themselves. The second responsibility is to help students understand their role in making the world better.

After working for many years in higher education, in 2009 I was appointed to the position of director of the Smithsonian National Museum of African Art in Washington, D.C. During the eight years that I worked there, I often thought about growing up in the South during a period when I was not welcome at museums, theaters, and concerts in downtown Jacksonville because of the color of my skin. I would also think about how fortunate I was to grow up in a home where my mother had what in the world of art is called "the eye." That is, she was not an art historian, nor was she an artist, but she had a natural appreciation for and understanding of the visual arts. And my family was truly fortunate to have the material resources for my mother to adorn our home with quality reproductions of great art, including works by African American artists.

I brought to my new professional involvement in the world of art museums the same concerns about diversity that I constantly posed about the world of higher education. Specifically, why is it that the majority of museums in the United States and around the world do not use the visual arts to tell the stories of all people? Why is it that only 9 percent of the visitors to art museums in the U.S. are people of color? Why were there no exhibitions in a major museum that focused on sexual difference until 2010, when the National Portrait Gallery presented *HIDE/SEEK: Difference and Desire in American Portraiture?* Why are there so few museums with accommodations for visitors who are blind or visually impaired, deaf or hard of hearing, or have other physical or mental challenges? Why is it that 46 percent of museum boards in the U.S. are all White? Why is it that despite the increasing numbers of women holding the top leadership role of director at U.S. museums, the larger the museum's budget the less chance there is that the director is a woman? And why is it that only 12 percent of the individuals in leadership positions in museums are people of color?

All of these questions paint a picture of how much work must be done to transform America's museums into places that are truly diverse, equitable, accessible, and inclusive. And yet in museums today there is a far greater awareness of the need for courageous conversations about race, racism, and other systems of inequality, and of the importance of follow-ing up such conversations with the kind of intentionality that includes an action plan. Much of this relatively new focus on the importance of greater awareness of and attention to diver-sifying museums is clearly the result of the work of two profes-sional organizations, the American Alliance of Museums and the Association of Art Museum Directors. And the Andrew W. Mellon Foundation has contributed mightily to this focus on the importance of diversifying museums by conducting two demographic surveys of art museum staffs.

The third arena in which I have worked involves consulting with businesses and not-for-profit organizations that express a commitment to transforming their workplaces into more diverse and equitable environments. Often a chief diversity officer plays a major role in efforts to bring about this kind of cultural transformation.

Convening courageous conversations about race, racism, and other systems of inequality has been in the toolkit of chief diversity officers for many years. However, following the 2016 presidential election, many diversity officers were faced with a new challenge—how to facilitate productive conversations among colleagues whose views on race, gender, religion, and other differences are strongly shaped by their allegiance to a political figure or political party. Diversity officers also indicate that the difficulty many of their colleagues are now having in finding common ground with others in their workplace is also true in terms of their families.

In his book *Our Search for Belonging: How Our Need to Con-nect Is Tearing Us Apart,* Howard Ross says this about these new challenges: "We are living in a society today that can feel at times like it is coming apart at the seams. For some this is mostly what they see on the news or in their social media platforms, because they live in environments that seem largely homogeneous. For others it is the day-to-day experience of living in communities that are torn between 'them' and 'us,' or in workplaces in which there is a constant, underlying nervousness about what we can and cannot talk about. Even within families, different political and social perspectives create tensions and separation."[1]

And yet, we must find a way to engage in difficult conversations with family members, with colleagues, with our neighbors, with those with whom we go to school, worship, and socialize. Why is it particularly difficult to have a courageous and productive discussion about race and racism?

I think there are several reasons. First, any meaningful conversation about race and racism in America must include an acknowledgement of enslavement. And that means not only confronting an institution that was intensely brutal, but also acknowledging that the long-ago ancestors of a White person in this conversation may have been slave owners—or at least did not oppose slavery. A courageous conversation about race and racism also requires talking about Whiteness and white-skin privilege. It is often exceedingly difficult for a White person who is not wealthy to accept that he or she is privileged, if for no other reason than being born White. A courageous conversation about race and racism can also be difficult because at some point, the person of color and the White person may feel that they have to defend everyone else of their race.

Another challenge in having a conversation about race and racism is that it is easy for White participants to draw a false conclusion: that ending racism, or even reducing the amount and extent of that system of inequality, is a zero-sum game.

That is, the thinking goes, if Black people gain rights, then White people will lose rights. It is not easy to spell out exactly how we can proceed to have far more justice and equity for everyone.

Courageous conversations about race and racism are also difficult because of the desire for quick solutions. Addressing—not to mention reducing—racism is a long-standing, complex, and incredibly difficult problem. I also think that it is tempting for White participants in such conversations to try to minimize the systemic nature of racism and "make things better" by declaring that when it comes to race, they are color blind. However, color blindness is something none of us is capable of achieving.

The final point I would make about the difficulty in having a courageous and productive interracial conversation about race and racism is that it is easy for White folks to focus on being guilty about racism, and for Black folks to speak only out of their anger. And yet, no matter how difficult this task is, what choice do we have if we want to engage in frank, open, and fearless conversations that require that all participants are respectful, honest, and willing to be vulnerable?

While race and racism is an exceedingly difficult topic to take on, to do so—as with any topic, including those that concern personal matters or religious beliefs—involves acknowledging the important role of information, of facts, of that which is documented. And there is much to be learned by examining any topic for discussion in a historical context. For example, to understand the challenges African Americans continue to face with respect to education requires going back to the period of enslavement, when laws were passed to prevent Black people from becoming literate, and when it was against the law for White people to teach Black people to read and write.

Anti-literacy laws were a major strategy used by southern slave owners to dehumanize and to control enslaved Black people. Despite the fact that many White southerners were not able to read or write, denying Black people the right to become literate was one more way of maintaining the myth of White supremacy. There were also practical and financial reasons for the anti-literacy laws, which included keeping important information away from the enslaved. As a Mississippi slave owner observed, knowledge and slavery are incompatible. And yet, in spite of all of the laws and efforts to keep enslaved people from learning to read and write, strategies emerged within the Black community to counter those efforts.

Today we see how racism continues to impact our educational system, with African Americans and other historically marginalized groups placed at a distinct disadvantage in overcrowded and under-resourced facilities. Racism also impacts our health care system. While poor and working-class families of all backgrounds often lack access to adequate health care, the combined impact of poverty and poor health care is deeply felt in Black and Brown communities, where obesity, hypertension, and infant mortality are disproportionately higher than among White Americans.

Structural racism also deprives Black people of competitive employment opportunities, and places them in neighborhoods where adequate housing and access to healthful foods and other amenities are lacking. In such situations, African Americans quickly become targets of predatory lending schemes that result in foreclosures and missed opportunities to pass along generational wealth.

Racism strongly impacts experiences of Black and Brown people within the criminal justice system, including racial profiling, police brutality, higher rates of convictions, and more oppressive sentencing. As a result of these multiple outcomes from systemic racism, a far lower value is placed on Black lives than on the lives of White Americans.

Our America is an extraordinary country. We have come a long way from the days of slavery, and we have made much progress since I first experienced racism as a little girl growing up in the segregated South. And yet much work remains to be done to give life to the dream that Dr. Martin Luther King Jr. so eloquently and powerfully articulated on August 28, 1963, as he stood on the steps of the Lincoln Memorial on the National Mall.

"Now is the time to make real the promises of democracy," Dr. King told the throngs of people who had gathered on the Mall. "Now is the time to rise from the dark and desolate valley of segregation to the sunlit path of racial justice. Now is the time to lift our nation from the quicksand of racial injustice to the solid rock of brotherhood. Now is the time to make justice a reality for all of God's children."

Dr. King was speaking about life in the 1960s and the failures of the U.S. government and the American people to live up to the constitutional principles of democracy, equality, and justice. Yet today, in some ways more than when Dr. King shared his dream, ours is still a divided house. We are divided along racial and ethnic lines, we are divided between haves and have-nots, we are divided in terms of the religion we practice, and we are divided on a wide range of issues—from what to do about the criminal justice system in our country to how to have a workable, fair health care system to how to address questions about abortion and immigration.

As Abraham Lincoln said on the eve of the Civil War, "A house divided against itself cannot stand." President Lincoln uttered these words five years prior to signing the Emancipation

Proclamation, which abolished slavery for African Americans who resided in the Confederate states. Although he came to be known as "the Great Liberator," the truth is that Lincoln, one of the greatest of our presidents, remained conflicted over the best course to pursue to sustain the Union. He knew that slavery was wrong, but influenced by the racist ideology of the times, he was not convinced that African Americans were equal to White Americans in anything other than their right to earn a decent living. This is why he initially proposed gradual abolitionism, hoping to mollify the fears of slaveholders who held fast to the notion that human beings could be held as property in perpetuity. Only the ravages of war and the Confederate recalcitrance forced his hand, resulting in the decision to support emancipation.

Who knows what course Lincoln might have pursued had he lived years beyond that horrible moment when he was assassinated. Indeed, it is important to note that Lincoln's understanding of race, like Thomas Jefferson's, was tainted by the racist ideology of White supremacy. Perhaps an important point to consider here is Lincoln's shifting views that helped pave the way for the full abolition of slavery. We must hold individuals accountable for racist actions and harmful views. But we also have to believe in the capacity of human beings to change.

It was in the wake of Lincoln's death that the Radical Republicans in Congress moved to adopt the Thirteenth Amendment to the Constitution, which abolished slavery. And with the Fourteenth and Fifteenth Amendments, African American men gained the right of citizenship and the right to vote, victories for which substantial numbers of Black men and women had fought and died. According to historian John Hope

Franklin, approximately 38,000 Black soldiers died over the course of the Civil War, although this number does not account for the civilians and other African Americans who offered up their lives with the hope that subsequent generations of Black people might enjoy freedom and first-class citizenship rights, including African American women.[2]

Despite their sacrifices, which during slavery included the forced bearing of children in order to replenish the workforce, African American women would have to wait a half century more, until the passage of the Nineteenth Amendment, to gain the right to vote. Even then, exercising that right would pose a real challenge for Black women as well as Black men who resided in southern states. As many White women claimed victory in the women's suffrage movement, Black women were largely excluded from the movement on the basis of their race, causing many of them, like Ida B. Wells-Barnett and Mary Church Terrell, to organize their own movement. Additionally, since many White suffragists deployed racist arguments to gain support for the Nineteenth Amendment among local legislators and Congress, it really was not until a century later, when President Lyndon B. Johnson signed the Civil Rights Act, that Black women and men could vote in large numbers. Oftentimes, the fortitude of African American women is overlooked in celebrations of advancements in the women's rights movement. This is yet another reason why it is critical that we seek to understand the ongoing impact of intersectionality on the life chances of historically marginalized groups.

In many ways, the passage of the Reconstruction amendments was a remarkable achievement. They helped to end more than 250 years of slavery in America, the "peculiar system" that impacted millions and that claimed millions of lives.

Additionally, Reconstruction offered many African American communities opportunities to make critical advances by way of politics and education. During the late 1860s and the 1870s, hundreds of African American men assumed political offices throughout the South, with many serving as legislators, lieutenant governors, state senators, and representatives. Among the notable leaders were Louisiana governor P. B. S. Pinchback and the first Black senators, Hiram R. Revels and Blanche K. Bruce of Mississippi. Unfortunately, after Revels and Bruce it would be nearly a hundred years before the nation elected the next African American senator, Republican Edward Brooke of Massachusetts.

Many congressional land grants also originated during Reconstruction, leading to the establishment of many of our historically Black colleges and universities (HBCUs), such as Howard and Fisk Universities and Spelman and Morehouse Colleges. It is to the HBCUs that we owe thanks for some of our outstanding leaders in the years after the Civil War. One of these leaders was Dr. Mary McLeod Bethune, a co-founder of the United Negro College Fund and the founder of Bethune-Cookman College, now a university. Other prominent alumni of HBCUs are physician Charles Drew, who pioneered research in the field of medicine; NAACP attorney and Supreme Court justice Thurgood Marshall; Dr. Martin Luther King Jr.; author Toni Morrison; philanthropist Oprah Winfrey; and scholar and activist Dr. W. E. B. Du Bois, one of the co-founders of the NAACP and the first African American to earn a doctorate from Harvard University.

Despite the advances, in the years immediately following Reconstruction African Americans witnessed an all-out assault on their nascent civil rights. It was as if "the slave went free; stood a brief moment in the sun; then moved back again toward slavery" is how Dr. Du Bois summed up the period in his seminal work, *Black Reconstruction,* which he published in 1935 in an effort to counter prevailing narratives suggesting that Reconstruction was a dismal failure.[3]

"The problem of the twentieth century is the problem of the color line," Du Bois had written more than 30 years earlier in *The Souls of Black Folk,* a book that should stand as essential reading in our schools. Du Bois believed that racism was the foremost challenge that confronted Americans during the century following Reconstruction. "The nation has not yet found peace from its sins," he wrote, observing: "The freedman has not yet found in freedom his promised land. Whatever of good may have come in these years of change, the shadow of a deep disappointment rests upon the Negro people."[4]

When Du Bois opined that following Emancipation, African Americans had stood for but a brief moment in the sun, he was referring to specific instances of racism that prevented them from capitalizing on their newfound freedoms. Indeed, he was referring to the systematic disenfranchisement of African Americans across the South, the consequence of White political betrayal during the Compromise of 1877, when Republicans withdrew from the South the protective devices that would ensure that African Americans could exercise their constitutional rights. Du Bois was also referring to sharecropping and the crop-lien system, practices that trapped many African Americans in cycles of dependency that made economic mobility very difficult, if not impossible.

As one of the anti-lynching activists of the era alongside Ida B. Wells-Barnett, Du Bois was also speaking about anti-Black violence and what were, for all intents and purposes, the foundations of mass incarceration in the United States. As I wrote in the first chapter of this book, between 1877 and 1950 close to 4,500 African Americans died at the hands of lynch mobs. Women and children were among those who were tortured, maimed, and killed as White citizens hoped to reestablish complete political, economic, and social control throughout the South.

There is documentation and photographs of the lynching of Laura Nelson and her son, L. D. Nelson, who were hanged from a bridge in a small town in Oklahoma in 1911. The two had been accused of murder. Before they could stand trial, a mob extracted them from their jail cells and carted them off to the nearby bridge, where several sightseers—including White women and children—gathered to see the mother and son hoisted over the edge and dangled below like trinkets on a keychain. After capturing images of the victims, photographers memorialized the lynching through postcards they sold. One photograph appears in the book *Without Sanctuary: Lynching Photography in America*.[5] To date, the photographs of Laura Nelson are the only ones of the lynching of a Black woman.

The Emmett Till Antilynching Act, which makes lynching a federal crime, carries the name of the fourteen-year-old African American youngster who was lynched in Mississippi in 1955. A similar bill was first proposed in 1900 and again in 1918, during the height of World War I, in which thousands of African Americans served and died. However, it failed to pass both houses of Congress. Despite ongoing protests from groups like the NAACP, in subsequent years the bill continued to suffer defeat. More than a century later, the bill to condemn lynching as a federal hate crime has yet to reach the president's desk for approval.

"I think it's important that there is an effort now to acknowledge this history and to do what we should have done a century ago," Bryan Stevenson of the Equal Justice Initiative argues. "A lot of folks will say, 'Well, it's not relevant today; it's not necessary today.' But lynching violence was created by politics of fear and anger, and we should never assume that an era of fear and anger will never occur again."[6] For this reason, we must have the courage to talk about a period in America when lynchings took place again and again in the North and the South, the East and the West. And at times, Mexican Americans were killed by this horrific means. We must also talk about the continuum that the Equal Justice Initiative draws from enslavement to lynching to mass incarceration.

During the eighteenth and nineteenth centuries, the value of Black lives was largely measured in terms of what price Blacks' bodies would yield at auction. Their designation as property was perhaps the only thing offering enslaved people some protection from racist Whites who wielded violent acts under the law, such as in the slave patrols, or "paddy rollers," whose job it was to police enslaved Blacks, most especially escaped slaves. Notably, it was during this time that the highest rates of lynching occurred as a form of White-on-Black violence.

In the years following Reconstruction, African Americans became the prime targets of racist policing practices. Where the newly established Ku Klux Klan could not reach, various other legally sanctioned practices could. For example, through what were known as vagrancy laws, Black people could be arrested for being "idle." Given the large-scale unemployment African Americans faced—having never been awarded their "forty acres and a mule"—many were charged with this offense.

Upon their arrest, many became subject to what was known as convict leasing, through which prisons hired out inmates to work for little or no pay. The practice has continued into modern times; as late as 1995 southern states like Alabama were hiring out prisoners to work in chain gangs. Today, many corporations rely on inmates as a cheap source of labor, with the prisoners paid pennies on the dollar for their work. It's a practice that Michelle Alexander calls "the new Jim Crow" in her book of the same name, and that others compare directly to slavery.[7]

No matter what we call it, here we see the unbroken line from slavery to lynching to mass incarceration. Today, the United States leads all other industrialized nations with high rates of incarceration. Since the beginning of the war on drugs, which President Richard Nixon began as part of his so-called War on Poverty, America's prison population has increased from 300,000 to more than 2.3 million.[8] According to research conducted by the NAACP, as of 2014, African Americans constituted 34 percent of the total correctional population, whereas Whites comprised 32 percent and Latinxs comprised 22 percent.[9] However, according to the 2018 census estimates, African Americans represent only about 13 percent of the population and Latinxs represent about 18 percent.[10] The NAACP notes that the imprisonment rate for Black women is double that of White women, and that African Americans account for 32 percent of arrests made among children. The organization also notes that African Americans are incarcerated five times as often as Whites. Thus, according to the NAACP, if African Americans and Hispanics were incarcerated at the same rates as Whites, prison and jail populations would decline by almost 40 percent.[11]

It is true that the criminal justice system ensnares poor and working-class people of all backgrounds. But like Nixon's war on drugs, the system unfairly targets Black communities through what historian Khalil Gibran Muhammad calls "the condemnation of Blackness" or the presumption of criminality, which dates back to the post-Reconstruction period. As Muhammad notes: "The link between race and crime is as enduring and influential in the twenty-first century as it has been in the past. Violent crime rates in the nation's biggest cities are generally understood as a reflection of the presence and behavior of the Black men, women, and children who live there."[12]

The presumption of guilt leaves Black and Brown people vulnerable to racial profiling by police, wrongful arrests, higher rates of conviction, and more extreme forms of punishment, including the death penalty. And children of color are disproportionately targeted to sustain the school-to-prison pipeline, with more extreme disciplinary measures that often result in lifetime prison sentences for the same behavior for which children of privilege receive but a slap on the wrist. As Muhammad points out: "In all manner of conversations about race—from debates about parenting to education to urban life—Black crime statistics are ubiquitous. By the same token, White crime statistics are virtually invisible, except when used to dramatize the excessive criminality of African Americans. Although the statistical language of Black criminality often means different things to different people, it is the glue that binds race to crime today as in the past."[13]

These are matters that we must be willing to talk about. As Ida B. Wells-Barnett wrote, "The way to right wrongs is to turn the light of truth upon them."[14] Wells-Barnett played a critical role in countering the presumption of criminality among lynch victims who endured a fate similar to that of Laura Nelson and her son. She challenged the prevailing trope that African Americans are more genetically predisposed to violence and crime than Whites and other racial groups.[15] When we "turn the light of truth" upon the wrongs of the past, there is so much about any conversation on race and racism that must wrestle with realities that range from difficult to horrific. The reality of all these dark moments and trends in American history discourages many from talking about them. And yet we must!

"Black history does not flatter American democracy; it chastens it," Ta-Nehisi Coates wrote in a 2014 essay for the *Atlantic* that staked out a case for reparations. "The popular mocking of reparations as a harebrained scheme authored by wild-eyed lefties and intellectually unserious Black nationalists is fear masquerading as laughter," he continued. "Black nationalists have always perceived something unmentionable about America that integrationists dare not acknowledge—that White supremacy is not merely the work of hotheaded demagogues, or a matter of false consciousness, but a force so fundamental to America that it is difficult to imagine the country without it."[16]

In other words, racism is so deeply imbedded in our history and our national psyche that integration alone—which in many ways speaks more readily to social conditions than it does to structural inequality—is not a sufficient remedy for the economic and social maladies that continue to afflict many Black communities. But, much like Germany's decision to grant several billion dollars in reparations to Israel on behalf of Jews who suffered during the Holocaust, reparations for African Americans may just help to tighten the wealth gap that disproportionately disadvantages Black communities.[17]

"And so we must imagine a new country," Ta-Nehisi Coates insisted in his essay, in many ways echoing the words of Abraham Lincoln during the Civil War. "Reparations—by which I mean the full acceptance of our collective biography and its consequences—is the price we must pay to see ourselves squarely. . . . What I'm talking about is more than recompense for past injustices—more than a handout, a payoff, hush money, or a reluctant bribe. What I'm talking about is a national reckoning that would lead to spiritual renewal."

In a surprising change of course, David Brooks of the *New York Times,* who often asserts conservative arguments in his writings, indicated that he now supports modern-day reparations for slavery. Brooks says he changed his mind after reading Coates's essay for the *Atlantic* and after traveling across America and witnessing firsthand our nation's vast racial disparities. He writes: "We're a nation coming apart at the seams, a nation in which each tribe has its own narrative and the narratives are generally resentment narratives. The African-American experience is somehow at the core of this fragmentation—the original sin that hardens the heart, separates Americans from one another and serves as a model and fuel for other injustices." He argues further that, as a move towards reconciliation, now is the time for us to consolidate all of the different narratives so that everyone feels a sense of inclusion in the fabric of our democracy. Moving beyond words, Brooks insists that we now offer a "concrete gesture of respect," which is necessary for us to begin anew. While he acknowledges that a national reparations agenda would be difficult to enact, he suggests that "the very act of talking about and designing [policies] heals a wound and opens a new story."[18]

Is Brooks serious? Many of his critics suggest that we hold our applause until we determine if he is merely offering lip service for a very pressing social justice issue.[19] Yet, a better question to ask is: How did David Brooks come to have this change of heart? We have to leave room for the possibility that people can alter their beliefs about racism as well as the underlying factors that keep racism alive, and this holds true for the most avowed racists as much as it does for White liberals. We are right to maintain skepticism, if for no other reason than to protect ourselves against the dangerous acts that racists commit. However, if Brooks is willing to entertain a different opinion about reparations, we have to believe that people are capable of change.

The movement among our LGBTQ siblings to gain recognition under the law and assert their rights as citizens and human beings is an example of how our society is capable of radical change. Influenced to a great extent by the strides that Black civil rights groups were making during the 1960s and '70s, during this same time activists involved in the gay rights movement became more vocal about the persecution they faced. These issues came to a head in June 1969 as a result of the Stonewall riots, after police targeted and raided a New York City establishment that catered to gay and transgender persons. In the weeks that followed, activist groups challenged the discrimination that LGBTQ people experienced, thereby igniting the gay liberation movement in the United States. One of the more prominent leaders in the movement was Marsha P. Johnson, an African American transgender woman who helped found the Gay Liberation Front. However, Johnson is often overlooked in the recounting of the history of gay transgender movements.

Over the next several decades, LGBTQ Americans continued to face a series of hardships, including employment discrimination and inequality under the law with regard to marriage. In 1993, the U.S. military enacted the infamous "don't ask, don't tell" policy whereby gay, lesbian, and bisexual individuals who hoped to join the military were forced to conceal a core part of their identity. The policy was repealed in 2011, only eighteen years after it was enacted. In 2015, the Supreme Court moved to protect same-sex marriages under the Fourteenth Amendment. Compare this radical shift to the Civil Rights Act of 1964 and the Voting Rights Act of 1965, designed to protected citizens from discrimination on account of race some seventy years after the Supreme Court legalized segregation under *Plessy v. Ferguson* and a century after the enactment of the Fourteenth and Fifteenth Amendments, which were supposed to guarantee citizenship and voting rights for African American men.

These days, it is difficult not to feel what seems like a backlash against the social progress we have made over the last century. Indeed, many in our country appear emboldened to openly express racism, anti-Semitism, and other forms of bigotry that we associate with the "Old South" and the pre–civil rights period. Following Barack Obama's election in 2008 as America's first Black president, many people believed or at least hoped that things would be different. The award-winning journalist Nikole Hannah-Jones wrote in the *New York Times* in 2016: "[A]s Obama racked up primary victories, not just in the expected cities but also in largely White Rust Belt towns and farming communities, it seemed evidence for many Americans that the nation had finally become 'post-racial.'"

She added: "Of course, that post-racial dream did not last long, and nothing epitomizes the naïveté of that belief more than the election last week of Donald J. Trump."[20] Following the presidential election in 2016, the bigotry that previously appeared latent began to rear its ugly head, demonstrating that America had not in fact entered a post-racial period. We quickly learned that the past was ever present in terms of bigotry around race and other expressions of human difference.

With these realities staring us clearly in the face, many remain unwilling to talk about race and racism in American life. For example, the Equal Justice Initiative reports that as of 2016, 38 percent of White Americans agreed that the nation has made the necessary changes to achieve equal rights. The research, which relies on the Pew Research Center polls, indicates that only 8 percent of African Americans believe that the country has made the necessary progress towards securing equal rights for all. The same study indicates that 41 percent of White respondents insist that we pay too much attention to race these days, and only 19 percent believe that institutional racism poses a bigger problem than individual prejudice, contrasting with 70 percent of Black respondents who see institutional discrimination as a significant factor in American life.[21]

In *The Burden: African Americans and the Enduring Impact of Slavery,* edited by Rochelle Riley, Torrance G. Latham wrote this: "Because the truth about American history does not make for palatable optics politically, Black and White children are robbed of learning uncomfortable truths about slavery and its residual impact when their minds are most fertile. . . . Meanwhile, the American government functions seamlessly as the predatory system designed to keep the public ill-informed, pro–Western civilization, and under control."[22]

In so many ways, it is a profoundly challenging time to be Black in America. Rather than celebrating the magnificence and strength of so many different kinds of people all living under one American roof, many in our country seem bent on returning us to a period when the nation was legally divided based on a myth about race, and racism was boldly practiced.

While African Americans have remained the primary targets of much of the racial hatred in our country, they are not the only targets. Immigration policies that privilege travel and citizenship for those originating from European countries while characterizing as criminals and rapists individuals who are seeking refuge from oppressive conditions in their countries south of the U.S. border are just one example that bears this out.

The way families from countries below America's southern border are held in detention centers, with parents often separated from their children, is reminiscent not only of the forced separation of Black families at the auction block, but of late-nineteenth-century policies like the Chinese Exclusion Act, which barred immigration from China despite the fact that Chinese immigrants were responsible for building our country's railroads, the very engines that promoted capitalist industry and wealth. We are also reminded of the inhumane conditions and treatments that Japanese Americans were subjected to in the internment camps in America during World War II. And we must never forget the horrific acts that occurred day after day during the Holocaust, resulting in the death of over six million Jews as well as members of other groups, including those deemed to be homosexual or mentally ill. Calls to construct a wall on our southern border remind me of a bygone era of repression, as exemplified by the physical and ideological walls various factions championed during the Cold War.

World War II and the Holocaust should have taught us an important lesson, namely, that it is important that we act swiftly against bigotry. Even if we are not directly impacted by specific forms of hatred against "the other" at a particular moment in time, as the privileged few seek to maintain power we might eventually find ourselves subject to the same forms of inhumanity. And, as Martin Niemöller warned us in the wake of the Holocaust, if we fail to speak out, when finally they come for us, there will be no one left to speak for us.

The strength and the long-term viability of our nation rest on the powerful idea that there is a place of respect in the American house for each and every one of us. And just look at us: What a people we Americans are! What a people we are in our full array of human diversity. Americans are folks of different races and ethnicities; we are women folks and men folks and transgender folks; we are different ages, religions, and sexual orientations; and we all function along a continuum of being abled and disabled.

And yet we have not yet found a way to talk about the realities of race and racism and the other ways that continue to divide us in our nation and our world. We have not learned how to respectfully interact with those who are different from us, including those who hold different political views. We have not yet proven to the satisfaction of all the power that people engaging across communities have to solve problems. We have not yet found the way to convince everyone in our nation that it is possible for different groups of people to maintain their distinctiveness and still work together for the common good. And we have not sufficiently illustrated the benefits of multiple ways of seeing and doing and being. There is a Chinese saying that so vividly captures this point: "One flower never makes a spring."

This climate of intolerance and divisiveness that is now so pervasive in our country demands that we re-dedicate ourselves to analyzing and understanding negative reactions to difference. And I do believe we can and must begin this process by having courageous conversations about race and racism—and indeed about all systems of inequality in American life.

How might Black people and White people sit down together and have courageous conversations about race and racism? I posed this question to Minal Bopaiah, my colleague in diversity work and the founder and principal consultant of Brevity and Wit, a strategy and design firm focused on helping organizations achieve change. Here are her ground rules for White people in such conversations:

1 The conversation must never be about winning. It must be about understanding and being understood. For that reason, present your arguments with your truth, not your intelligence.

2 Talk about your own privilege and victimization in the same breath.

3 It will be helpful if you have a good understanding of what empathy is. While we like to say it is about putting yourself in another person's shoes, that is easier said than done. But what you can surely do is to believe people of color when they share their experiences.

4 Listen more and talk less. Believe what people of color are saying.

5 When you tell your story of success, be sure to acknowledge that far more than hard work got you to where you are. Talk about your journey to success by naming the schools, institutions, parents, communities, peers, mentors, tax laws,

health-care options, and other causes and conditions that contributed to your success.

Building upon Minal Bopaiah's suggestions, I propose the following ground rules for African Americans who want to engage in a courageous conversation with White Americans:

1 The conversation must never be about winning. It must be about understanding and being understood.

2 Talk about ways in which you constantly experience victimization and marginalization. But also describe ways in which you have some privilege.

3 It will be helpful if you have a good understanding of what empathy is. As difficult as it may be to put yourself in a White person's position, do your best to do so. Now, as you imagine having white-skin privilege, ask yourself and the person you are conversing with these questions: What would it take for you to give up white-skin privilege? What can you imagine as a better way to live?

4 As you speak about your constant experiences with bigotry and systemic racism, do your best to remember these words of Bryan Stevenson: "Each of us is more than the worst thing we've ever done."

5 When you tell your story, do not shy away from discussing the hardships you have experienced because of racism. But be sure to also share what you have nevertheless accomplished, and the joy there is in being a Black person.

As we continue to find ways to have courageous conversations about race and racism, I offer an African proverb and an African American saying that should encourage us to talk across the racial lines that divide us. The African proverb says: "An ant on its feet can do more than an elephant lying down." So let us not feel powerless to have these conversations. The African American proverb says: "A closed mouth gets no food." Let us open our mouths in respectful talk with each other about race and racism. Doing so may well begin to feed our souls and help us to make progress toward that day when difference does not make any more difference.

3

IMAGINE OUR NATION WITHOUT RACISM

A Call for Action in the Academy

Not everything that is faced can be changed, but
nothing can be changed until it is faced.
—*James Baldwin*

THE CIVIL RIGHTS MOVEMENT of the 1950s and '60s did not
end racism in America. Nor did racism in America end with
the election of Barack Obama as the first African American
to serve as president of the United States. In fact, the years
between Dr. Martin Luther King Jr.'s assassination in 1968
and Obama's election in 2008 were filled with racial confla-
grations that shook cities across our country. Following the
assassination of Dr. King in Memphis, where he had gone to
offer support to striking sanitation workers, at least a hundred
cities were engulfed in flames, including Chicago, New York,
Detroit, Baltimore, and the nation's capital. The uprisings were
a direct reflection of the anger African Americans felt over the

assassination, and of their ongoing frustration with how slowly they were seeing any lessening of the stranglehold that racism had on their lives.

With the 1965 Watts riots and a long history of police brutality etched in local memory, Los Angeles in 1992 again became the center of prolonged protest when a jury acquitted the four officers who had been caught on video beating an unarmed and utterly defenseless Rodney King. These "race riots," as they were called, compelled many Americans to question whether the civil rights movement had made any fundamental changes in race relations in the United States. And the questioning continued: Why were African Americans still on the bottom rungs of America's racial caste system?

Years later, following the 2016 presidential election, these same questions were posed in response to the unleashing of particular expressions of racism that had lain dormant—and that many had hoped were a relic of the past. In part because of the use of the internet, White hate groups gained greater visibility and, to an extent, enjoyed greater tolerance than in the post–World War II years.

Then there were the events of August 11 and 12, 2017, in Charlottesville, Virginia, that captured the attention of our country and the world. Racial violence broke out during a Unite the Right rally that drew hundreds of White nationalists and neo-Nazi demonstrators to the city to protest the removal of a statue of the Confederate general Robert E. Lee from a park.

Armed with tiki torches, Nazi flags, shields, sticks, pepper spray, and even guns, the demonstrators shouted "White lives matter!" along with various anti-Semitic slogans. They also mimicked monkey sounds to express their alignment with the racist notion that Black people are subhuman. They were met by a large body of University of Virginia counter-protestors and civil rights activists, with whom they clashed over the course of two days. Both sides experienced injuries. The counter-protestors suffered a fatality after an avowed White supremacist rammed his car into a crowd, killing thirty-two-year-old Heather Heyer and injuring many others.

Speaking about the event only a few days after the violence, President Donald Trump said, "I think there is blame on both sides. You had a group on one side that was bad. You had a group on the other side that was also very violent. Nobody wants to say that. I'll say it right now. . . . I've condemned neo-Nazis. I've condemned many different groups. Not all of those people were neo-Nazis, believe me. Not all of those people were White supremacists by any stretch."[1]

Similar incidents of racial hatred and aggression had taken place over the course of many years prior to the events in Charlottesville. Two years before that public display of racial hatred and violence, Dylann Roof, a twenty-one-year-old White supremacist, murdered nine parishioners who were attending a Bible study at the Emanuel African Methodist Episcopal Church in Charleston, South Carolina. For many Americans, this horrific act of racial violence brought back memories of September 15, 1963, that profoundly tragic day when the Sixteenth Street Baptist Church in Birmingham, Alabama, was bombed, killing four young African American girls: Carol Denise McNair, eleven years old, and Addie Mae Collins, Cynthia Wesley, and Carole Robertson, all fourteen years old.

A White nationalist movement in the United States is linked to a series of racist and anti-Semitic terror attacks. The Southern Poverty Law Center documented 940 hate groups in the United States in 2019, with a 55 percent increase in White nationalist hate groups and a 43 percent increase in anti-LGBTQ hate groups since 2017. There is also the increasing boldness with which some members of society display their antipathy towards anyone or anything they regard as different. And many individuals feel emboldened in ways reminiscent of the Dixiecrats of old, whose politics were shaped by an attachment to segregation and White nationalism.

The politics of division and fear that characterizes much of our current sociopolitical climate is also present on college and university campuses. In late February 2018, during Black History Month, a resident of a dormitory at Eastern Michigan University discovered a Black doll that had been hung from a shower rod. One student living in the dorm suggested that the doll was placed there as a "prank" and was not meant to be racist or malicious. During the previous month, a University of Oklahoma student posted a video on social media that showed a White woman student filming another as she placed black paint on her face and spoke the words "I am a nigger" into the camera.

A year later, numerous instances of White people donning blackface surfaced, including the revelation that while attending Eastern Virginia Medical School, Virginia governor Ralph Northam had posed in blackface for a photo with another student proudly boasting Ku Klux Klan regalia. The photo appeared in the 1984 yearbook. Other politicians, including Alabama governor Kay Ivey, had to grapple with their own blackface scandals.

A review of 900 yearbooks for 120 colleges revealed more than 200 additional examples of racist material inscribed in the books, according to *USA Today*.[2] Similar expressions of bigotry have occurred on high school campuses. In reaction, one set of students at the Ethical Culture Fieldston School in Riverdale, New York, started a lock-in as a form of protest against their administration's handling of racist incidents at the school. The responses by school administrators to such incidents have differed. Some have offered apologies for the actions of their students, and in writing at least they have re-affirmed their commitment to diversity and their promise to promote safe spaces for all students.

These particular instances of bigotry taking place in high schools and on college campuses reveal how racism is so often a part of the academic culture in the United States. And of course, what takes place in schools, colleges, and universities often reflects what is taking place in the larger society. Again, in what seems to be an increase in incidents since the 2016 presidential election, Black Americans are the targets of White people racially profiling them for actions so seemingly innocu-ous as grilling in a park or patiently waiting for friends at Star-bucks. Such incidents have led Black Americans to develop a list of everyday actions for which they are often harassed by police "while Black"—including "driving while Black," "eating while Black," "shopping while Black," and "walking while Black."

In the spring of 2018, Yale University was the site of an incident involving a student "napping while Black." A White graduate student, Sarah Braasch, called the police on Lolade Siyonbola, a Black graduate student in the African studies department, after she found her sleeping in a common room in their dorm. Although Siyonbola's books and notes were visibly spread out on a table, Braasch nevertheless decided that the student had violated building policy by sleeping in the room, something exhausted graduate students are known to do. "I have every right to call the police," Braasch insisted, while snapping a photo with her cellphone. "Get my good side,"

Siyonbola responded, assuring the police when they arrived that "I have every right to be here." According to Siyonbola, Braasch had acted similarly two and half months prior when she discovered a Black man, a friend of Siyonbola's, in the stairwell.

Responding to the event, Yale president Peter Salovey said: "Racism is an unqualified evil in our society. Universities are not utopias, and people of color experience racism on our campus as they do elsewhere in our country. This fact angers and disappoints me. We must neither condone nor excuse racism, prejudice, or discrimination at Yale."[3]

As each of the foregoing examples reveals, our educational institutions are not shielded from the ideology and practices of racism. Indeed, colleges and universities often function as microcosms of the broader society. And yet, we must do more than acknowledge that racism impacts our lives and all of our institutions. Let us begin by posing and responding to this question: Why are there still such serious challenges to diversity, equity, accessibility, and inclusion on college and university campuses?

For answers, we must look to the history of higher education, as well as the ways our educational systems developed alongside and within the context of racism. And we need to acknowledge that while our higher education institutions can and often do promote racism, they also can help us study, understand, teach about, and convene courageous conversations about race and racism.

During most of the history of American higher education, it was tilted to the elite, and specifically elite men. Schools of the Ivy League and others that originated with the founding of our nation sought to exclude women, African Americans, and other historically marginalized groups. Except to the extent that these marginalized groups worked as slaves or as domestics in the schools' employ, universities and colleges reserved what they considered to be "the privilege of education" for the sons of the rich and powerful.

Many of these schools were successful primarily because of their institutional investment in the slave trade, as Craig Steven Wilder has outlined in his critical work, *Ebony and Ivy: Race, Slavery, and the Troubled History of America's Universities.* "The founding, financing, and development of higher education in the colonies were thoroughly intertwined with the economic and social forces that transformed West and Central Africa through the slave trade and devastated indigenous nations in the Americas," Wilder writes.[4] The academy never stood apart from American slavery—in fact, it stood beside church and state as the third pillar of a civilization built on bondage.[5]

This was true of schools in the North as well as in the South. Although the northern states were in the process of abolishing slavery in the early decades of the nineteenth century, during which time participation in the international slave trade also became illegal, schools like Brown, Harvard, Princeton, and Yale continued to benefit from a direct attachment to slavery. As with Thomas Jefferson's University of Virginia, which he founded in 1819, these schools also served as the breeding grounds for racist ideology governing the treatment of Black and indigenous peoples. These belief systems impacted various fields of study, including philosophy, theology, sociology, history, the natural and medical sciences, and economics.

It was not until the post–Civil War years that systems of education began to proliferate for "the common man." However, these schools developed at a relatively slow pace in the South, where there was less of a commitment to public education overall. Only four years after the Confederate army laid down its arms in the face of a Union victory, our nation also began to witness a paradigm shift toward much of what we know today as the American university. In 1869, Charles Eliot, then president of Harvard, shifted the vision of American higher education from pedagogy steeped in recitation and classical Greek and Latin to an elective system of courses.

These curricula included deeply important but presently endangered courses in the humanities, such as history. Of course, at the time, the type of history that students learned was often influenced by racism and a belief that "the White man's history" was superior to all other history, and that in some cases, White people were the only ones who possessed what could be properly labeled as history. As Carter G. Woodson, "the father of Black history," noted in *The Mis-Education of the Negro:* "The oppressor . . . teaches the Negro that he has no worth-while past, that his race has done nothing significant since the beginning of time, and that there is no evidence that he will ever achieve anything great."[6] Woodson's words, written in 1933, were echoed in the writings of other African American scholars such as W. E. B. Du Bois and Anna Julia Cooper.

During the late eighteenth and nineteenth centuries, the Black pioneers in higher education were a small cadre of women and men. Among them were graduates of colleges such as Middlebury in Connecticut, Bowdoin in Maine, Amherst in Massachusetts, and Dartmouth in New Hampshire. During this same period, a few Black students attended what is now Cheyney University of Pennsylvania, the first historically Black college, and Rush Medical College in Chicago. According to the *Journal of Blacks in Higher Education,* before the end of the Civil War, at least forty Black students had graduated from colleges and universities, all located in the northern part of the United States.[7]

It was during the post–Civil War years that many schools admitted Black students for the first time. Harvard, which had rescinded the admission of three Black students in 1850 after some pressure from White students who attended its medical school, awarded degrees to Black students in dentistry and law in 1869. In 1870, the first African American received an undergraduate degree from Harvard. Twenty-five years later, Harvard would graduate its first African American doctoral student, the sociologist and civil rights activist W. E. B. Du Bois.

In 1874, Rev. Patrick Healy, who was born a slave, the son of an Irish Catholic planter and an enslaved mulatto woman in Macon, Georgia, became the president of Georgetown University. He was the first person of color to hold such a position in a predominantly White university, and he did so even as public schools remained segregated in the nation's capital.[8]

The 1800s also marked the emergence of women's colleges—Mount Holyoke, Vassar, Wellesley, Smith, Spelman, and others. Oberlin, a liberal arts college established in Ohio in 1833 and my alma mater, played an important role in the abolitionist movement and in 1835 was the first four-year institution to admit African Americans. In 1844, Oberlin graduated its first Black student, George B. Vashon, one of the first professors to work at Howard University upon its founding in 1867.

In 1837, Oberlin also admitted women, becoming the first coeducational college in our nation. Though Black women had previously attended Oberlin, upon graduating from there in

1862, Mary Jane Patterson became the first African American woman to earn a bachelor's degree from any American college or university. At one point in her career, she served as the first principal of M Street High School (later renamed Dunbar High School) in Washington, D.C. Oberlin continued to educate a number of outstanding Black professionals, educators, and civil rights activists, such as Fanny Jackson Coppin, Anna Julia Cooper, Mary Church Terrell, John Mercer Langston, and Senator Blanche K. Bruce. Unlike Oberlin, many schools continued to exclude African Americans, some as late as the mid-twentieth century.

The Seven Sisters began admitting African American women in small numbers beginning in the mid-1880s. Even when they consciously admitted Black students, these women's colleges often enforced discriminatory policies. In 1927, the president of Smith informed a parent that while the college had no right to exclude Black women, "we take care that a colored girl and a White girl never have to share the same room, and we advise colored girls for their own comfort to room outside the college."[9]

In the same year that the president of Smith used polite language to express what was clearly a discriminatory policy, the following happened to a young African American woman named Dorothy Irene Height. After applying to and being accepted at Barnard, a women's college in New York City, she arrived to begin her classes only to be told that Barnard had already reached its quota for Black students. Refusing to be deterred from receiving a college education, she applied to, was accepted, and enrolled at New York University, where she earned two degrees: a bachelor's in education in 1930 and a master's in psychology in 1932. Dr. Height went on to become a preeminent champion of civil rights and women's rights, leader of the National Council of Negro Women for close to fifty years, and a recipient of the Presidential Medal of Freedom and the Congressional Gold Medal. When I work at her desk in what had been her office in the Dorothy I. Height Building, headquarters of the National Council of Negro Women, I often think about her refusal to give up her seat in a higher education institution. Her persistence was surely a factor in placing her in the role of being the only woman to stand alongside the six national civil rights leaders: Dr. Martin Luther King Jr., John Lewis, A. Philip Randolph, Whitney Young, James Farmer, and Roy Wilkins. At the March on Washington in 1963, Dr. Height was the only woman to sit on the stage with the six leaders; however, she and no other women were allowed to speak—a clear bow to patriarchy.

As schooling continued to develop in the nineteenth century, federal land grants became an important source of funding for schools. In many ways, programs like the Morrill Land-Grant Act served as an extension of the Reconstruction Amendments that abolished slavery and guaranteed suffrage and citizenship to African American men. However, while the Morrill Act introduced a more utilitarian model of higher education, some scholars argue that, contrary to conventional views, the land-grant colleges did not appreciably democratize higher education. Ongoing practices of racial exclusion only impressed upon many African Americans the need to pursue educational opportunity apart from the institutions that promoted beliefs about Black inferiority.

The mid-1800s gave rise to colleges and universities founded by freed people and White philanthropists who made full use of land grants. These schools challenged the presumption that only Whites could or should be educated. Thus the nineteenth century witnessed the founding of historically Black colleges and universities, including Wilberforce University in Ohio (1856), Fisk University in Nashville (1866), Morehouse College in Atlanta (1867), Howard University in Washington, D.C. (1867), Hampton Institute in Virginia (1868), Bennett College in Greensboro, North Carolina (1873), Spelman College in Atlanta (1881), and Tuskegee Institute in Alabama (1881).

As Dr. Roslyn Clark Artis, the current president of Benedict College, a historically Black college in Columbia, South Carolina, pointed out: "Our nation's historically Black colleges and universities are the living, breathing manifestation of the African American lived experience in this country." Echoing the words of Carter G. Woodson, she continued: "Our schools bear living witness to the fact that a thorough understanding of our own history leads to positive self-image, academic and social success, as well as professional and economic prosperity for people of color."[10] Historically Black colleges and universities account for a high percentage of the undergraduate and graduate degrees earned by African Americans.

According to the National Center for Education Statistics, during the 2017–18 school year, approximately 327,000 students attended the 101 public and private HBCUs located throughout the United States and the U.S. Virgin Islands. Those identifying as Black comprised 76 percent of the student body and accounted for 74 percent of the degrees conferred that year.

Historically Black colleges and universities clearly play a critical role in the education of African Americans, many of whom choose to attend these institutions because they receive a quality education in an environment that is largely free of racism. In terms of post-undergraduate studies, three-quarters of all African Americans who earn a Ph.D. do their undergraduate work at an HBCU. While historically Black colleges and universities account for only 3 percent of America's four-year higher education institutions, their alumni account for 80 percent of the country's Black judges and 50 percent of Black lawyers. HBCUs account for 25 percent of Black undergraduates who earn degrees in STEM fields (science, technology, engineering, and mathematics).[11]

In recent years, the number of Black students attending HBCUs has decreased. Although Black attendance rates remained relatively steady at HBCUs between 2010 and 2018, at predominantly White colleges and universities Black enrollment rates more than doubled.[12] There are several possible explanations for these realities. There was a general decrease in college attendance overall (7 percent among all students). The situation might have been partially due to the widening of opportunities for Black students at predominantly White institutions that offered attractive scholarships. Another factor could well be the financial hardship and ever-increasing debt at both the institutional and individual levels. As Dr. Artis observed: "[T]hese institutions [HBCUs] teeter on the brink of extinction due to unyielding economic pressure. If these valuable treasures are permitted to die, a significant piece of our history will die with them."[13]

Despite the ongoing marginalization and exclusion of people of color in higher education at the turn of the twentieth century, by the 1920s there was increased democratization in higher education. Influenced by the philosophy of the nationally renowned Progressive Era educators like John Dewey, colleges and universities began to open their doors to all classes of Americans, signaling the ongoing shift from an elite system to one that was more deeply invested in educating individuals from across all economic levels. Nevertheless, in the South, "separate and unequal" racist practices meant that African Americans were still excluded from many of these institutions.

Even in the 1930s, when civil rights lawyers began to step up their activism against Jim Crow schooling and pressure school administrators to provide equality of opportunity in higher education, many schools responded to these calls by propping up ramshackle facilities or paying for Black students to attend schools elsewhere.

The case of Lloyd Gaines is an example of the resistance to integrated schools. After graduating in 1935 from Lincoln University, a historically Black institution in Jefferson City, Missouri, Gaines, an African American, applied for admission at the University of Missouri Law School. (Lincoln did not have its own law school.) The university refused his admission on the basis of "separate but equal," and the state vowed to erect a law school for Gaines and other Black students to attend in the near future. Unmoved, Gaines appealed the decision in the courts, and in the subsequent landmark case, *Gaines v. Canada* (1938), the Supreme Court ruled that the university had violated Gaines's Fourteenth Amendment rights, or "equality under the law."

In writing a dissenting opinion, one justice argued that education was an issue that should be left to the states, not the federal government. Since Missouri had been willing to pay Gaines's tuition for an out-of-state law school, this meant that he still had access to an education equal to that of White law students. Before either theory could be worked out, Lloyd

Gaines disappeared, never to be seen again. Responding to the newfound threat of integration, many White schools and educational systems included Black schools in their line items for their next year's budget, though many of the schools were never established.

In other instances, Black people were uprooted from the only homes they knew, simply because colleges and universities continued to exclude them. According to Pennsylvania State University professor Crystal Sanders, who is currently completing a book on Black southerners' efforts to secure graduate education during the era of legal segregation, "During [this time], southern and border state legislatures relegated African Americans to limited undergraduate educational opportunities at severely underfunded tax-supported Black colleges. Public graduate and professional school education was virtually nonexistent. To comply with the Supreme Court's 1896 separate-but-equal doctrine, these states sent thousands of young African Americans to the other regions of the country for the post-baccalaureate education that White citizens received in state. Southern and border states purported to offer Black and White citizens the same graduate opportunities, although only Black students had to leave the place of their birth to receive graduate training."[14]

The three decades following World War II ushered in a new period of expanded opportunity at all levels of education. More and more African Americans and other historically marginalized groups also gained access to schools that once promoted their exclusion. In 1954, the Supreme Court ruled in *Brown v. Board of Education* that the practice of segregating public schools is unconstitutional. The following year, in *Brown II*, the Supreme Court directed schools to desegregate "with all

deliberate speed." Responding to the slow pace of desegregation and the mounting White resistance, ten years later Title VI
of the Civil Rights Act prohibited discrimination in schools
based on race, color, or national origin. Enacted in 1965, the
Elementary and Secondary Education Act emerged as a central piece of legislation under President Lyndon B. Johnson's
War on Poverty. The act provides funding for local schools in
socioeconomically disadvantaged areas. That same year, the
Higher Education Act authorized federal aid for postsecondary
education. The subsequent decade witnessed challenges to
discrimination in schools based on sex and disability.

During the 1960s and '70s, social and political issues were
at the center of activism on college and university campuses.
It was during this period that large numbers of concerned
students and faculty challenged higher education to broaden
its original mission. They stressed the need for a type of research and teaching that would address America's complex
social problems—especially those that centered around race
and socioeconomic status.

Initially, the civil rights movement did not seem to pose a
threat to higher education. The demand for access seemed to
be no more than a request for a seat at the table or a chair in
the classroom. However, it was not long before it became clear
that schools cannot exist apart from the political and social
contexts that drive institutional decision-making. In the 1960s
and '70s, college students were determined to make their voices
heard about matters related to American race relations, the U.S.
war in Vietnam, women's and LGBTQ rights, free speech, and
nuclear armament, among other issues.

Black students specifically called for the recruitment of
more diverse faculties and curriculums that reflected racial

and socioeconomic diversity; and they also pressed for the allocation of resources towards these ends and demanded that institutions provide them with a type of education that reflected the changes taking place in their evolving world. Not surprisingly, it was in the '60s and '70s that the nation witnessed the flowering of new academic programs that were designed to do just this. Black studies programs and departments were formally institutionalized in the 1960s as a result of Black student activism, as Martha Biondi indicated in her critical exploration of the period, *The Black Revolution on Campus:* "With remarkable organization and skill, this generation of Black students challenged fundamental tenets of university life. They insisted that public universities should reflect and serve the people of their communities; that private universities should rethink the mission of elite education; and that historically Black colleges should survive the era of integration and shift their mission to community-based Black empowerment. Most crucially, Black students demanded a role in the definition and the production of scholarly knowledge."[15]

As Biondi chronicled, in 1968, Black students held a five-month strike at San Francisco State College to demand a Black studies program. Soon after, the college established its first Black studies department. Protests like the one in San Francisco also took place at Northwestern University, at Brooklyn College, and at Howard University, resulting in the establishment of Black studies programs at various institutions.

The late 1960s also witnessed the emergence of women's studies programs. In 1969, Cornell University developed the nation's first fully accredited women's studies course. Cornell was simultaneously the center of Black student activism, as students also demanded a Black studies program. San Diego

State established the first women's studies program in 1970, although the first women's studies Ph.D. program came much later, in 1990, at Emory University.

During the late 1960s and '70s, many colleges and universities also witnessed the flowering of Chicano studies, Puerto Rican studies, Asian studies, and other ethnic studies programs. Since then, and due in great part to the prolonged commitment of pioneering activists who were determined to broaden representation in the curriculum and the student body, a host of new courses, certificates, and degrees focusing on experiences of historically marginalized groups have emerged.

In recent years, as illustrated by the tragic events in Charlottesville in 2018, higher education has become embroiled in controversies over the placement of Confederate statues on various campuses. On one side of the debate, there are those who claim that the statues are part of our American heritage. "So this week, it is Robert E. Lee," President Trump offered in the wake of the Charlottesville protests. "I noticed that Stonewall Jackson is coming down. I wonder, is it George Washington next week? And is it Thomas Jefferson the week after that? You know, you really have to ask yourself, where does it stop?"[16]

On the other side of the debate are those who insist that the statues remain as testaments to a past filled with racial hatred, anti-Black violence, and economic exploitation. And every time a Black student or student of color sits down in a library to study or walks across the college green to relax, the statues are there to serve as reminders of their racial exclusion, reminders that they don't belong. "When one's sense of human dignity is on the line, one can never demand enough," historian Tikia K. Hamilton observed in 2015 in the aftermath of protests taking place at Princeton, where students hoped to have a statue of former U.S. and Princeton University president Woodrow Wilson removed. Though many regard Wilson as an exceptional president for his statesmanship during World War I, others point to his record of racism, wherein he promoted the resegregation of federal government, praised the racist film *The Birth of a Nation,* and endorsed the idea of racial inferiority of individuals still caught in the grip of White imperialism. In addition, Hamilton noted, "the demands of [the] student protestors align well with America's democratic traditions, the very basis upon which our nation was built. It is ahistorical to regard their efforts outside of this great American tradition."[17]

Some schools have worked to remove statues, or at least to listen to the concerns of faculty and students who stand on both sides of the debate. Nevertheless, there is a prevailing myth among many political conservatives that our colleges and universities are overrun with liberal efforts to transform them into places that are hardly recognizable from the institutions that once excluded people like me. However, that is not true. When we look at the composition of higher education, we know the change has not been that drastic.

For example, according to the National Center for Statistics, in the fall of 2017, White men and White women comprised about 76 percent of all full-time faculty in degree-granting postsecondary institutions, compared to 23 percent for everyone else. When looking at the most senior faculty (full professors only), racial disparities are the greatest: White men and White women accounted for 81 percent, while Black and Hispanic professors accounted for 2 percent. The numbers for more junior faculty are only slightly better: Among assistant professors, White men and White women accounted for 72 percent, while Black and Hispanic assistant professors accounted for 4 percent.[18]

The rate of college enrollments seems to offer room for optimism, but these numbers can be characterized as somewhat deceptive. The period from 1976 to 2010 witnessed an explosion in the rates of attendance among the general population of students, but beginning in 2010, these numbers began to decline. This suggests that there is still work to do.

We must also consider retention rates, as well as the experiences and opportunities afforded to students after they graduate. As the most recent research indicates, while students who identify as Asian or Pacific Islander tend to graduate at a rate exceeding that of most other racial groups, Black students graduate at a significantly lower rate than all other groups, including Latinxs.[19] We must address this significant question: As we recruit African Americans to our institutions, what are we doing to ensure that they succeed? Furthermore, in what ways might we transform our colleges and universities to ensure a more inclusive and equitable experience for everyone, so that they continue to excel after they graduate?

As Anthony Abraham Jack points out in his recent work, *The Privileged Poor: How Elite Colleges Are Failing Disadvantaged Students:* "There's a difference between access and inclusion. Universities have extended invitations to more and more diverse sets of students but have not changed their ways to adapt to who is on campus."[20]

To address the problem of inclusion and thus retention, Jack suggests that institutions become thoughtful and creative in their solutions, such as teaching students how to utilize campus resources, like professors' office hours and mental health and career services; addressing food insecurity issues; and even keeping facilities open during holiday breaks so that students who cannot afford to return home have a place to stay. By and large, the problems of mental health and other needs that are unaddressed in many historically marginalized communities remain unaddressed when students come to colleges and universities. This is often the consequence of fears about exposing any degree of vulnerability within racially hostile and often elite environments.

"Dissemblance" is a term many Black scholars have used to describe the behavior of African Americans who try to disguise any perceived weaknesses, and this includes showing emotions. In response to dissemblance, universities and colleges need to become more creative in how they help students to overcome these challenges, including hiring more service providers that have diverse backgrounds.

When calling for colleges and universities to actively engage in transforming their institutions into more diverse, equitable, accessible, and inclusive environments, it is helpful to simply make the case for why this should be done. We can borrow from how some corporations lay out the case for this kind of transformation.

First, there is the moral case. That is to say, it is the right thing to do to bring students of diverse backgrounds (some of whom are diamonds in the rough) to our colleges and universities and to hire and retain qualified faculty, staff, and administrators.

Corporations also say that in order to carry out their mission—which of course is centered on being profitable—in an increasingly diverse world requires that they bring into their workforce people of various backgrounds who will come with different, innovative, and ultimately profitable ideas. This is called the business case for diversity. I like to put a twist on this and speak of a pedagogical case for diversity. By this I mean that in order for colleges and universities to carry out their mission—which is to prepare students to make a good living and no less importantly to live a good life in our highly technological and diverse world—campuses must consist of diverse people in their student body, faculty, staff, and administration. In addition, the curriculum must move away from what my colleague at Spelman College Dr. Beverly Guy-Sheftall calls "the three Ws"—western, White, and womanless. This is to say that the curriculum must be centered in teaching and learning about the multiplicity of the world's peoples, their histories, and cultures.

Having made the moral and pedagogical case for diversity and inclusion in American higher education, now the question is how to do this. Following are three actions that colleges and universities can take toward this goal.

First, they should courageously guard liberal arts education against the ongoing attacks to undermine more than a century's worth of progress. Nationwide, we continue to witness an assault on liberal arts education and particularly the humanities, which is the bedrock of a type of education that retains as its central goal the education of citizens towards a more democratic society.

There is much in Mercer University's ongoing dedication to the liberal arts and the humanities that is truly exemplary. According to the university's core curriculum guidelines: "A hallmark of a Mercer education is that students take interdisciplinary courses to build strong academic skills while exploring interesting ideas and texts." Mercer offers an integrative curriculum, which combines traditional disciplines with multidisciplinary courses that allow students to explore their own identities and other cultures through the arts. Students can major in Africana studies and women's and gender studies; and as part of Mercer's focus on experiential learning, students are encouraged to participate in service learning projects and study abroad programs. I deeply admire Mercer's slogan: "At Mercer, everyone majors in changing the world."

Unfortunately, unlike at Mercer, some universities across the country are in the process of downsizing their offerings in the humanities, merging departments or eliminating liberal arts majors altogether. Much of this has to do with a "bottom line" approach to education, where colleges view students as consumers who are merely interested in the types of educational programs that can ensure that they will enjoy lucrative careers in an evolving economy. Some refer to this as "academic prioritization." As Linfield College English professor Reshmi Dutt-Ballerstadt writes: "The term is increasingly being employed, in theory and in practice, by administrators at liberal arts colleges and universities across the country to explain or justify decisions to cut certain programs or even entire departments. Such decisions are essentially a death sentence for the liberal arts. It is a simultaneous devaluation of the many underrepresented, first-generation and social justice–oriented faculty (who were hired as a result of various diversity initiatives) who teach in disciplines such as foreign languages, women's and gender studies, area studies, critical race and global studies, etc."[21]

In light of these trends, academic institutions must be brave. Rather than de-emphasizing the humanities, institutions must re-emphasize them. They must re-emphasize the importance of history, literature, interdisciplinary studies, African American studies, women's studies, and queer studies. And I strongly believe our academic institutions must champion the study of anthropology. Each of these program areas has the potential to play a role in reshaping conversations and actions about race and racism.

Secondly, in order for colleges and universities to actively engage in efforts to address racism in the academy, White faculty must work to raise their own consciousness and engage in the kind of study and human empathy that will permit them to teach and treat all students, including students of color, in fair and effective ways. As Audre Lorde once said, if Black professors can teach Shakespeare and Emily Dickinson, White professors can learn to teach James Baldwin and Zora Neale Hurston.[22] To be well-educated and informed, students need to read, explore, and critique Shakespeare and T. S. Eliot. But students should do no less with the works of Langston Hughes and Toni Morrison. To learn of Chinese American life, students should be introduced to the works of Maxine Hong Kingston; and reading the works of Rudolfo Anaya and Sandra Cisneros can contribute to their appreciation of Chicano and Chicana life and culture. To better understand Native American women's realities, students can be directed to read Joy Harjo and Paula Gunn Allen.

Finally, we must charge the leadership of predominantly White institutions to bring people of diverse backgrounds to their campuses and not to give up until they have recruited and retained students, faculty, staff, and administrators who reflect the diversity of our country and our world. Diversity in education requires that the very participants in this great process of teaching and learning are of different backgrounds, and institutions must create inclusive environments that are critical for retaining diverse student populations, faculty, staff, and administrators.

As I imagine a world without racism, I offer the following bold steps that colleges and universities can take if they are to play a meaningful role in the creation of such a world.

What if, in every school, college, and university, every student was required to take a course on the history of race and racism in America?

Imagine if all students were incentivized to participate in various interdisciplinary studies programs that examine racism, sexism, heterosexism, and other systems of inequalities, instead of allowing these programs to languish on the margins of our academic communities.

Similar to Mercer's experiential learning program, imagine if every student was required to spend time working, studying, or residing in a country, culture, or community other than his or her own. Imagine the degree to which such experiences could expand students' worldviews and prepare them to live more joyously in our highly diverse world.

Imagine if all faculty, staff, and students were required to participate in effective unconscious-bias training programs. And imagine if all of our colleges and universities found a way to have groups of faculty convene conversations about race and racism in churches, synagogues, temples, mosques, and community centers.

If our educational institutions cannot serve as sites where racism is explained and challenged, where else will this happen? But, of course, we must have the will for this to happen and to struggle to make it happen. In thinking about the possibility of drastic, necessary change and social transformation,

I conclude this book with the words of the great abolitionist and feminist Frederick Douglass: "The whole history of the progress of human liberty shows that all concessions yet made to her august claims have been born of earnest struggle. . . . If there is no struggle there is no progress. Those who profess to favor freedom and yet deprecate agitation are men [and, let us add, women] who want crops without plowing up the ground; they want rain without thunder and lightning. They want the ocean without the awful roar of its many waters. . . . Power concedes nothing without a demand. It never did and it never will."[23]

AFTERWORD

Enter to learn; depart to serve.
—*Mary McLeod Bethune*

You have to act as if it were possible to radically
transform the world. And you have to do it all the
time.
—*Angela Davis*

Growing up during the 1980s and '90s, I always looked to
education as a way of catapulting me beyond the social and
economic disparities that engulfed my all-Black neighborhood
on the South Side of Chicago. With six children forced to share
a three-bedroom apartment, I knew that we were not the
poorest family on our block. I don't recall ever going without
three square meals a day; nor do I remember extensive periods
where we lacked heat, hot water, or clothing, even if the latter
necessitated my mother rummaging through endless piles at
the Salvation Army, and me peeping around corners to ensure
that none of my friends had spotted us. Additionally, there was
no shortage of books in our apartment. All around us, stuffed
along makeshift shelving and inside recycled milk crates, was

the opportunity to gain knowledge of new words and ideas, offering expedited travel to distinct and faraway lands.

Nevertheless, in my mind, something about the way we lived was not normal. Whether it was the condition of our dwellings—which included an apartment overrun with mice—the outdated textbooks and dilapidated school buildings, or the increasing crime that resulted in the incarceration and, in some cases, the loss of neighborhood friends, our collective circumstances seemed unfair, unjust even. Powerless to alter the conditions around me, I set upon education as a vehicle for mobility—a way out, so to speak. Very quickly, I learned that education could do things for me as a little Black girl. It could gain me praise, visibility, and leverage among teachers and peers, especially since people often treated me as an outlier among those whom society regarded as mere statistics. It could serve as a form of escape from family troubles and offer me a ready excuse against peer pressure. "I can't today, I have to take a test" was sometimes (though not always) the response I offered when friends encouraged me to skip school. "As long as I'm back before my test," I proposed as a fair compromise between toil and trouble, especially when cute and charismatic boys were involved. Yet, no matter whether I was babysitting my younger siblings, sneaking off with friends, or working nearly full-time hours throughout high school, I always prioritized earning high marks. The pursuit of education helped shape my very identity as a young Black woman.

Soon, my perseverance landed me nearly a thousand miles from home at a liberal arts college in the quaint town of Hanover, New Hampshire. In many ways, my time at Dartmouth College provided a real culture shock. So much about the place was different from what I had previously experienced. Set amid rolling green hills under a seemingly endless blue sky, the campus was beautiful, serene, and mostly safe for anyone who avoided frat culture, which was a given for most Black students at the historically White college. Although the small dorm room that I initially shared with roommates may have appeared meager to them, the accommodations were a vast improvement over the bed I once shared with my two younger sisters. The mere sprinkling of color that I detected among a sea of White faces required a bit of an adjustment, sure. However, other aspects of my experience nearly compensated for the sense of alienation I may have felt as one of a relatively small number of African Americans attending the school.

In English, African studies, and my various other classes, I learned to expand the scope of my thinking to the point where I often felt as if my mind were exploding. I learned how to engage close readings of classic texts such as Plato's *Republic* and Shakespeare's numerous plays. I became acquainted with gender politics in various African societies, while gaining exposure to African art, history, and culture. Readings and course discussions also fueled a strong desire to learn more about the world beyond the classroom, leading to a greater appreciation for racial, ethnic, and class diversity, including the wide diversity that characterizes the Black diaspora. Participating and serving as a leader in various student organizations helped to plant in me the seeds of a lifelong commitment towards addressing issues of social justice, especially where the experiences of historically underrepresented groups are concerned. Through a domestic exchange program, I enjoyed the opportunity to attend Spelman College for a semester, which is where I met Dr. Johnnetta B. Cole some twenty-five years ago. Additionally, my fondness for world travel to some of the least-trodden places also began in college, as part of graduation requirements that involved foreign language study in Spain.

My liberal arts education served as the foundation for deep analysis and critical thinking in all manner of areas. Yet, it was my developing passion for the study of history that forever altered my perspective. Upon leaving Dartmouth, history is where I committed most of my career and my pursuit of lifelong learning, perhaps the most important objective that a liberal arts education can fulfill, as Dr. Cole has so eloquently captured in the foregoing pages. Although several decades divide our experiences, much like Dr. Cole and a legion of African American women and men before us—including my maternal grandmother, who combined work as a teacher and as a domestic in White homes, and my mother, who earned a bachelor's degree in education while caring for six children—I also have carried this commitment into other areas of my life, including teaching and research.[1]

Like education, my engagement with Black history also has come to mold my identity. But not only that, my exposure to the aspirations, challenges, and achievements of my ancestors has served as an anchor in times of trouble and doubt, offering me a worldview that is unique to Black women, as the scholar-activist Anna Julia Cooper insists in *A Voice from the South,* a text that should stand as required reading in schools, alongside various other classics. A graduate of Oberlin College, Dr. Cole's alma mater and the first college to open its doors to African Americans in the nineteenth century, Anna Julia Cooper was the fourth Black woman to ever earn a Ph.D. Channeling the resilience that so many Black women have exhibited in a world in which racism conspires with patriarchy against our best interests, Cooper achieved this remarkable feat at the age of sixty-seven. In 1892, while pondering the importance of higher education among Black women, as well as the deep implications of the "race problem" that confronted Americans at the turn of the twentieth century, she wrote: "But to be a woman of the Negro race in America, and to be able to grasp the deep significance of the possibilities of the crisis, is to have a heritage, it seems to me, unique to the ages."[2] At a time when White women and several leading Black men claimed exclusive insight and authority in the realm of politics, Dr. Cooper believed that Black women had an especially important role to play by helping to move the country forward towards more progressive ideals. For Cooper, higher education would stand as a conduit through which all women could promote these ideals.

It is true—my liberal arts education has vastly influenced my worldview; it has carried me full circle from my early beginnings in Chicago, exposing me to ideas, people, and places that I might never have dreamed of as a little girl. "This is almost surreal," I recall thinking several years ago, while leading a talk at a massive lecture hall at Princeton, where I earned a Ph.D. in history. Standing before the wooden lectern and peering out over a predominantly White audience, I asked myself how it was possible that I, a Black woman who was raised in poverty, now commanded the attention of students at one of the nation's top schools.

The answers to this question are twofold, having everything to do with hard work and, perhaps to an even greater degree, providence, or what some might refer to as luck. Like many African Americans, particularly those who stem from economically disadvantaged backgrounds, I worked twice and often three times as hard as my White peers to achieve goals denied the majority of our Black friends and family members.

Yet, for all of our diligence, we have had to learn that hard work alone is insufficient to overcome the structural forms of racism that Dr. Cole describes in her three lectures. No matter our number of degrees or the size of our bank accounts, Black people still face discriminatory housing practices, discriminatory hiring policies, and vast disparities in wealth accumulation. As Dr. Cole outlines in her discussion of the behaviors we engage in "while Black" (such as "driving while Black," "sleeping while Black," and, as in the recent case in New York City's Central Park, "bird-watching while Black"), African Americans continue to face racial microaggressions at work, at school, and in our own neighborhoods. The renowned Harvard professor Henry Louis Gates Jr. learned this in 2009 when police arrested him for allegedly breaking into his own house in the predominantly White city of Cambridge, Massachusetts. Armed with degrees from Harvard and Columbia (also one of my alma maters), President Barack Obama, who mediated a meeting between Gates and the arresting police officer, was subjected to all types of racist vitriol during his time in office, including the slurs of colleagues. So too was Chicago native and Ivy League graduate Michelle Obama, whom detractors likened to an ape, a term of derision that dates back to nineteenth-century scientific racism. The Obamas' experiences in and beyond the White House prove that, all too often, race trumps educational attainment.

Despite it all, Black people have maintained a deep, historic attachment to the belief in the liberatory value of education, so much so that they have often risked violent reprisal and even death in the pursuit of it. "The presence of literate slaves threatened to give lie to the entire system [of slavery]," historian Heather Andrea Williams reveals of the antebellum period.

"Reading indicated to the world that this so-called property had a mind, and writing foretold the ability to construct an alternative narrative about bondage itself."[3] With these deeply held convictions in mind, African Americans established their own schools, and in the South, many did so well in advance of White citizens who placed a limited value on education for the masses. Undeterred by limited resources, they often gathered together paltry earnings in the hopes that future generations would gain more than just rudimentary skills and knowledge. Various public schools, along with Spelman, Fisk, Howard, and other historically Black colleges that Dr. Cole describes, were the results of their efforts. So too were the freedom schools of the civil rights period and the private schools that African Americans founded under the pan-Africanist and Black nationalist movements of the 1960s and '70s.[4] Additionally, Black activists' campaigns to gain community control over public schools during this time also reflected their deeply held beliefs about the importance of self-determination, a vision that extended beyond the classrooms and into community life more broadly.

Nevertheless, Black people have been forced to acknowledge that, in more ways than not, America is nowhere close to the meritocracy the White framing fathers envisioned in the early days of the republic, when they systematically denied Black people equal educational opportunity. Perhaps more than any other group in this country, African Americans have had to fight like hell against the belief that we are somehow less intellectually capable than anyone else. To White men such as the slaveholding Thomas Jefferson, the Benjamin Bannekers and Phillis Wheatleys of our society were intellectual aberrations—anomalies that required certification by their

White contemporaries to prove that they were capable of such genius, as Ibram X. Kendi describes in heralded scholarship that interrogates racist ideology across two centuries.[5] Additionally, where African Americans demonstrated remarkable ability and enterprise by operating their own schools and institutions, they were stamped nonetheless with the "badge of inferiority," which served as the underlying premise of *Plessy v. Ferguson* and other practices that relegated Black and White students to "separate and unequal" schools during the Jim Crow period. Stereotypes about Black inability also contributed to educational disparities in the decades following *Brown v. Board of Education,* amid a concerted backlash against desegregation among White families.

Even now, Black people are forced to swallow the hard pills of a Protestant work ethic and a bootstrap mentality that rarely places them in a position to compete with those who enjoy a century or more's head start over them. "A people thus handicapped ought not to be asked to race with the world, but rather give all of its time and thought to its own social problems," W. E. B. Du Bois insisted, referring to the post-Reconstruction period, when the federal government abandoned most African American families to their own devices, imposing upon them the daunting task of securing land, employment, education, and measures of protection against anti-Black violence.[6] A century later, President Lyndon B. Johnson echoed these sentiments after helping to usher in the Civil Rights Act of 1965, which outlawed discrimination based on race, color, sex, religion, and national origin. Prior to that, Black people had been largely excluded from federal entitlement programs that provided a buffer against economic hardship, including the Social Security Act and other New Deal programs established under

Franklin Roosevelt's administration. Despite the denial of entitlements to Black people during the 1930s and '40s, ever since the enactment of Johnson's various Great Society programs Black people have been positioned as the face of affirmative action. Likewise, they have been demonized as ready abusers of a social welfare system that has long trailed European advances, due in part to racial prejudice that characterizes Black welfare recipients as "welfare queens."[7] Yet, for all the hoopla that exists around welfare and affirmative action, by and large White Americans benefit more readily from these programs, legacies, and networks that ensure their advantage under America's opportunity structure, and that often abet their admission to the nation's top schools and cushy, well-paying positions upon graduation. A quick glance at the names on many campus buildings around the country help to reveal as much, along with the portraits of scowling White benefactors who seem to be placed there as reminders to African Americans and other students of color that they don't belong. The "Varsity Blues" scandal of 2019, wherein various celebrities paid upwards of $25 million to facilitate the admission of their children to top colleges and universities, stands as an even more egregious example.

As illustrated by prevailing attitudes towards entitlement programs, poor and working-class African Americans are often the more obvious targets of overt and structural racism. Nevertheless, educational pedigree provides little shield against the more overt forms of bigotry, such as racial profiling and police brutality. In this way, racism becomes as much of a life-or-death issue as it was in the days of slavery and Jim Crow, when White lynch mobs often murdered African Americans precisely because they dared to defy the racist social order and achieve success through entrepreneurship and other endeavors, as the journalist and anti-lynching crusader Ida B. Wells-Barnett uncovered. The Texas murders of Botham Jean and Black Lives Matter activist Sandra Bland, as well as Xavier University graduate Atatiana Jefferson, illustrate this point. So too does the recent police shooting of former University of Kentucky student Breonna Taylor in Louisville. For this reason, many educators are forced to combine the hard truths of history with the harsh dose of our present reality, especially for Black students, as Georgetown professor and award-winning educator Marcia Chatelain reveals. "Every year, I teach Black students who are hopeful that pursuing an education at an elite school will mean that their futures are secured, and more importantly, the indignities of racism will not visit their doors," explains Chatelain, who also has written extensively about Black economic self-determination and the limits of Black capitalism as a panacea for racial disparities in her acclaimed work, *Franchise: The Golden Arches in Black America.* "I try to be honest with them that their education has the potential to expand the number of choices ahead of them and it may provide some financial comfort, but at the end of the day, White supremacists are not interested in their resumes."[8]

African Americans of varying backgrounds also face extreme disparities in health care, as Chatelain illustrates in her discussion of the fast-food industry and obesity rates in primarily working-class Black communities. Yet, in the case of many African Americans, wealth provides little immunity from the racism that underlies the health care system. For instance, in 2018, the all-star tennis player Serena Williams's near-death experience while giving birth to her first child helped call attention to the reality that Black women are between three and four times more likely to die from pregnancy-related complications as White women, according to the Centers for Disease Control and Prevention.[9] Lack of access to adequate resources and information accounts only partially for these disparities. As historian Deirdre Cooper Owens observes in *Medical Bondage: Race, Gender, and the Origins of American Gynecology*—which details how White doctors subjected enslaved women to medical experimentation on the false ideological basis that Black women can withstand pain more readily than White women—a history of racism in the health profession accounts for these unnecessary deaths, as well. The refusal of health authorities to take Black women's concerns seriously also serves as a factor in the disproportionate death rates.[10] In fact, these dilemmas are what prompted public health care advocate Ashlee Wisdom to launch the Health in Her Hue campaign, which connects Black women with culturally competent health care providers who center Black women's lived experiences as part of their praxis. Notably, Serena Williams actively supports the Health in Her Hue initiative.[11]

Our varying experiences under the coronavirus pandemic help to bear out all too clearly the health disparities that Black people face, demonstrating further the ways in which race trumps class, as Dr. Cole argues. As I write, America and the world are battling a global pandemic that has killed more than one million people worldwide, according to recent data, although that number most likely will have increased by the time of publication.[12] In the United States alone, more than 200,000 people have died from COVID-19, due in great part to a shortage of medical supplies and a sluggish response on the part of the Trump administration, both of which have hastened the spread of the virus. Nevertheless, statistics currently highlight how, in cities around the country, the coronavirus has killed a higher percentage of African Americans than any other group. In Chicago, where I currently reside, the numbers are striking. While Black residents comprise 30 percent of the city's population, they currently account for between 60 and 70 percent of COVID-19 fatalities.[13] In Michigan, Louisiana, and the city of Milwaukee, where African Americans also represent a minority population, Black people are dispropor-tionately impacted by the virus. In these instances, poverty and a previous lack of access to adequate health care are proving deadly. Additionally, similar to many Latinxs, who are deemed "essential workers" only in a time of crisis, being forced to make a decision between the loss of life and the loss of a minimum-wage job that often lacks health-care benefits has landed many Black victims in the morgue.

Arguably, poorer African Americans seem to be more at risk of contracting this deadly illness than their more formally edu-cated counterparts. However, since those already experiencing preexisting conditions, such as high blood pressure, diabetes (both of which run in my family), and asthma, face a greater risk of dying, it is not surprising that college students and other white-collar professionals are being counted among the dead. Meanwhile, even in education, the coronavirus is helping to expose other racial inequities. As schools have moved to online learning platforms, which they hope will limit the disruptions taking place in grade schools, colleges, and universities every-where, it is becoming apparent that some students have more ready access to the internet and computers than other students. And since research has revealed that students of color, and particularly African Americans, are more likely to occupy the less affluent end of the digital divide, it is not difficult to imagine the additional burdens being placed on students, parents, and teachers of color who are attempting to navigate the uncertainties of the pandemic.[14] Meanwhile, the "reopening" of schools and businesses also portends a dangerous impact on Black and Brown communities, where the rate of COVID testing remains disproportionately lower than in White communities. Prioritizing the U.S. economy over American lives, this likely explains why White Americans have been at the forefront of protests supporting reopening.

As I sit writing from the comfort of my home during this pandemic, I am aware of my own privilege as an African American woman who has spent a great deal of my academic trajectory teaching in and attending elite and predominantly White schools that boast exponentially more resources than the public schools that I once attended, or the historically Black colleges that my niece recently attended in rural Mississippi or the one her brother currently attends in a small Ohio town. Yet, because the pandemic will undoubtedly deepen the preexisting economic divide between Black, Brown, and White citizens, it is important that we not conflate educational attainment with financial security or overall well-being. On average, educated African Americans have never enjoyed parallel degrees of financial security with their White counterparts. The sociologist E. Franklin Frazier argued as much in 1957 in his controversial book *Black Bourgeoisie,* wherein he attempted to call attention to the social and economic precarity of the Black middle class.[15] Anna Julia Cooper argued similarly when she observed: "We too often mistake individuals' honor for race development and so are ready to substitute pretty accomplishments for sound sense and earnest purpose."[16] For this reason, many African Americans find themselves "alone at the top," often as a consequence of hard work, but also as part of half-hearted efforts by predominantly White institutions and corporations to offer the appearance of diversity.

This is not to suggest that many formally educated African Americans have not accomplished extraordinary things that have allowed them to amass great wealth and provided them with opportunities to invest in institutions and programs that benefit Black people as a whole. Philanthropists such as Oprah Winfrey and the late Reginald F. Lewis, a Harvard Law School graduate and the first African American to build a billion-dollar business, are proof. Yet, in the whole history of the African American experience, ingenuity and courage oftentimes have counted as much as dignified letters. Such was the case of former domestic Madam C. J. Walker, who defied racism to become one of the first Black millionaires and whose fictionalized story appears in *Self Made,* a recent television series. Emerging as a powerful voice during the coronavirus pandemic, the singer and cosmetic industry titan Rihanna represents an important contemporary example, along with basketball superstar LeBron James and—despite the NFL's earlier attempts to blackball him for his stance against police brutality and other forms of racial injustice—Colin Kaepernick.

Hard times and the whims of the American economy cut across race, gender, and class, as Dr. Cole notes in her discussion of the Great Recession of 2008. Nevertheless, as she points out, the recession impacted African Americans disproportionately, including college-educated Blacks who can ill-afford to sell homes in the distant suburbs due to unequal rates of recovery, making it impossible for them to return to the city and compete financially with predominantly White gentrifiers. Add to this recent financial hardship the previous debt they may have incurred as a result of the high rates of tuition (especially for advanced degrees), and many African Americans find that they are only nominally middle class. As Georgia congresswoman and Yale Law School graduate Stacey Abrams acknowledged, "I finished my higher education deeply in debt and with seven years of bad credit in my future."[17] On top of the educational debt that Abrams still owes, she also has taken on some financial responsibility for her parents and a young niece who moved in with Abrams's parents after the child's own parents could no longer care for her. "Nearly twenty years after graduating, I am still paying down student loans, and am on a payment plan to settle my debt to the IRS. I have made money mistakes, but I have never ignored my responsibilities; I will meet my obligations—however slowly but surely," she added. Such is the case for so many African Americans who have staked a great deal of money on schooling in an economy that saddles young people with debts they may never be able to repay (myself included). Meanwhile, still reeling from the effects of foreclosure and unemployment, African Americans will most likely bear the brunt of the economic downturn that is accompanying the coronavirus pandemic. Consequently, African Americans, who have accumulated substantially more debt than any other group (including educational debt, according to the Brookings Institution), will continue to confront financial insecurity for the foreseeable future.[18]

The unfortunate truth is, for all of our individual accomplishments as Black people, education alone has never been sufficient to eradicate the type of racial degradation that accompanied two and a half centuries of slavery and a century-plus more of Jim Crow. As Dr. Cole observes, racism is imbedded in the very fabric of our development as a nation, and the field of education has not been immune to racist ideologies that both sanctioned and encouraged Black underdevelopment. This is one of the reasons why the educator Carter G. Woodson, who is regarded as the "father of Black history," encouraged a type of education that instilled in African Americans an affinity and a sense of obligation towards society's most vulnerable—more specifically, African Americans. "Real education means to inspire people to live more abundantly, to learn to begin with life as they find it and make it better," Woodson wrote, while he simultaneously challenged more highly educated Blacks to adopt the skills and ideals that would help them undermine racism.[19] In this way, Woodson also echoed the advice of one of the nation's greatest leaders, Mary McLeod Bethune, who founded Bethune-Cookman College (now University) and the National Council of Negro Women: "Enter to learn; depart to serve." Today, Bethune's words serve as the college's motto.

I agree with Dr. Cole when she cites Nelson Mandela: "Education is the most powerful weapon which you can use to change the world." Still, as she also notes, while education can plant the seed, perhaps what matters most is the type of education one pursues. Beyond instilling the facts of a particular episode in history or the ability to dissect the most foreboding classical texts, an education that privileges critical thinking is, above all else, the type of education that we can use to change the world. This is especially important in the age of "fake news" and other unreliable media, which are greatly undermining our democratic processes in the United States. An education that compels students to look around their college campuses and note the various ways majority populations are interacting, as compared to the ways underserved populations may not be interacting, will be the most effective tool in altering the racial disparities that still face

African Americans long after we seize hold of our hard-won diplomas and degrees. An education that builds in students an unmitigated commitment and the courageous pursuit of equity and justice will help us confront society's most difficult problems—including, but not limited to, the disproportionate rates of poverty, homelessness, and incarceration among African Americans and Latinxs; unequal access to quality health care; and the vast disparities in education. A truly intersectional education that also calls upon African Americans to confront many of the internal challenges in our communities—such as the homophobia, transphobia, and sexism that often result in high rates of anti-Black violence and suicide—is the only one in which we will actually be able to claim that, among us, all Black lives do indeed matter.

For these reasons, we must continue to help students bridge the gap between their course studies and what is occurring in the surrounding communities. As Bianca Baldridge, a sociologist and the author of *Reclaiming Community: Race and the Uncertain Future of Youth Work,* reminds us: "Schools are not, have never been, and will never be the only site for learning."[20] This holds true especially among Black students, who often view their schools and campuses as racially hostile environments. "Within Black communities (in homes, formal, and informal community-based educational spaces), youth work exists in a fugitive space—always fighting for a right to exist within the oppressive structures of anti-Blackness," Baldridge adds. Thus, a truly liberal arts education will also take into consideration the weight that Black students and other students of color carry with them to campus, with a nod to the fact that they are often dealing with so much more than course work and even financial insecurity; often, they are grappling with what it means to survive in a context where their lives don't yet seem to matter.

Fortunately, the protests that have accompanied the COVID pandemic, primarily as a response to the recent spate of police and White vigilante killings, provide much optimism for the future. The tragic murder of George Floyd, the Black Minnesota resident whom police officers suffocated in broad daylight due to his alleged passing of a counterfeit twenty-dollar bill, has reignited the Black Lives Matter movement in ways comparable only to the civil rights movement, demonstrating the degree to which Americans of all walks have been lulled out of complacency around issues of racial justice. Despite the ongoing ravages of the pandemic, protestors have risked their lives to demand justice for Floyd and for Ahmaud Arbery (who was "jogging while Black" in Georgia), Breonna Taylor ("sleeping while Black" in Louisville), Rayshard Brooks ("napping while Black" in Atlanta), and an ever-expanding list of victims of anti-Black violence. "[E]ven in the midst of this pandemic and social distancing and self-isolation, [people] are going to fight for a different kind of reality," observes Keeanga-Yamahtta Taylor, Princeton professor and author of *From #BlackLives-Matter to Black Liberation*. "And the struggle on the streets has to be turned into organizing, [and it] has to be turned into a set of achievable demands, but it begins with resisting the status quo and letting it be known that we're not all just going to lay down and die and accept this kind of meager existence that is being hoisted upon us."[21]

Meanwhile, in Senegal, France, South Korea, the Netherlands, Germany, and on at least four continents, millions of people have joined in solidarity with the Black Lives Matter movement, while also exposing much of the racism that transcends national boundaries and that continues to live and breathe as the direct byproduct of European colonialism and anti-Black prejudice in Asian, Latin American, and Arab countries, too. Not only that, the proliferation of protests around the world has helped call attention to other forms of racism, such as the racism that hides conveniently beneath the cloak of neoliberal agendas focused on preserving White privilege under the status quo—including that which White women have long enjoyed, as historian Stephanie E. Jones-Rogers chronicles in scholarship focusing on White women slave owners, and as I also highlight in research that examines how Black women battled racism during the woman suffrage movement.[22] The overt and structural racism that characterizes American education, both higher and secondary, has come under attack. Schools are being called to account for their indifference to the experiences of Black and Brown students and faculty, as reflected in their recruiting and hiring practices; their racially hostile campus environments; their willingness to favor White mediocrity over Black excellence; their flexible policies towards perpetrators of racism; and curricular objectives that continue to privilege White voices and experiences over the historically marginalized, among other things.[23]

In responding to "the voices of the unheard," as Dr. Martin Luther King Jr. characterized Black political rebellion in the 1960s, institutions have been forced to revisit questions about their complicity in perpetuating racism and racial inequality. Several years ago, during a thirty-two-hour sit-in led by Princeton University's Black Justice League, the 274-year-old institution refused to heed student demands to abandon Woodrow Wilson as the namesake of the university's graduate school of public policy.[24] In a quick turn of events, Princeton now has decided to drop the name of the bigoted university and U.S. president from the school. The Woodrow Wilson Fellowship Foundation is following suit. As incubators of inequality and bastions of White supremacy, various other schools—including many elite, predominantly White secondary schools—are undergoing scrutiny for similar reasons, prompted in great part by courageous students, faculty, and alumni who dream of better conditions for the next generation than those under which they suffered.

All around the country and the world, symbols of racism and imperialism, such as buildings bearing the name of the infamous slaveholding politician John C. Calhoun and statues boasting the conquests of the genocidal explorer Christopher Columbus, are taking a beating. Even statues of men like Theodore Roosevelt, Thomas Jefferson, and George Washington—often regarded as champions of democracy against the paradox of their racism towards people of color—are at risk of being toppled. While various conservative and liberal voices have criticized these protests—most especially what they regard as the "destruction of property" and the banishing of racist names and statues to historical obsolescence—others applaud the efforts. "Those who rebuke violent responses to injustice should ask themselves: How should the oppressed respond to their oppressors?" asks Kellie Carter Jackson, author of *Force and Freedom: Black Abolitionists and the Politics of Violence,* in an article for the *Atlantic*. "Throughout history, Black people have employed violence, nonviolence, marches, and boycotts. Only one thing is clear—there is no form of Black protest that White supremacy will sanction. Still, Black people understand the utility of riotous rebellion: Violence compels a response," she argues, although it is important to point out that diverse groups of people have been participating in these protests.[25] Challenging the racism of Donald J. Trump, Black leaders have demanded more than just symbolic change and measures designed to capitalize on "law and order" discourses that present African Americans as pathologically driven to crime while clearly pandering to conservatives, as Chicago mayor Lori Lightfoot discerns of President Trump's recent focus on "Black-on-Black" crime in the city. The "defund the police" movement is one prominent example of the push for tangible, life-altering results. Though perhaps merely a gesture, Washington, D.C. mayor Muriel Bowser's renaming of a section of a street in front of the White House, once the site of notorious slave pens, as the Black Lives Matter Plaza remains quite remarkable, given our nation's tortured relationship with racism. Each day that passes offers reassuring evidence that "change" is no longer simply a campaign slogan, as it was for Barack Obama in 2007–8. It's becoming reality.

"If we have the courage and tenacity of our forebears, who stood firmly like a rock against the lash of slavery, we shall find a way to do for our day what they did for theirs," the educator, activist, and college founder Mary McLeod Bethune insisted, while placing heavy emphasis on the ability and courage of young people, such as those who attended Bethune-Cookman College and those for whom she advocated as a leader in the National Youth Administration under President Franklin Roosevelt. Notably, Bethune was also the founder and president of the National Council of Negro Women, which works to empower Black communities and which Dr. Cole now heads. In the years ahead, we will face many challenges; and as we head into the 2020 presidential election, it is important that we maintain the optimism of both of these NCNW presidents, a century apart, who under slightly different contexts battled against some of the worst forms of racism (and sexism) to lead and sustain institutions and leave a vast and positive impact on the world.

Optimism plus vigilance is what will allow us to move beyond the most racially divisive moments in recent memory and ensure that we do not arrive at a moment of such vast inequality ever again. To do that, we must become more familiar with the challenges of the past so as not to continuously repeat the error of inattention and apathy towards the problems that plague society's most vulnerable populations. We cannot be content to return to business as usual, but instead we must adopt the attitudes of our forebears who understood that the survival of democracy demands constant struggle. "Nature has made up her mind that what cannot defend itself, shall not be defended," Anna Julia Cooper insisted, quoting Ralph Waldo Emerson. In this way, the turn of the twentieth century thinker demonstrated the breadth of her scholarship as a contemporary of W. E. B. Du Bois and one of the nation's first public intellectuals, as Black feminist scholar Brittney C. Cooper argues.[26] "What cannot stand must fall," Anna Julia Cooper continued, "and the measure of our sincerity and therefore of the respect of men [and women], is the amount of health and wealth we will hazard in defense of our right."[27] Such is true for the nation as a whole as it is true for African Americans.

As Anna Julia Cooper advised, more than my "pretty accomplishments," I am forever grateful for the "sound sense and earnest purpose" that my education has instilled in me. Were it not for the liberal arts, I am not sure that I would possess the knowledge or wherewithal to be able to "grasp the deep significance" of the ongoing crises that impact us all, or the possibilities that await us if we fearlessly and fiercely move towards more radical reform in our communities and institutions. Were it not for my liberal arts education, I would not have benefited from so many opportunities, which included my participation in the exchange program twenty-five years ago at Spelman, where I also studied history and, most important, where I met Dr. Cole.

I am deeply moved by Dr. Cole's generosity, vision, and enduring commitment to social justice, and I am honored by the opportunity to work with her and to share the insights that I could have only dreamed of as a little Black girl so many years ago.

TIKIA K. HAMILTON

NOTES

INTRODUCTION

1. Tim Carmody, "Without Jobs as CEO, who speaks for the arts at Apple?" *WIRED,* August 28, 2011. https://www.wired.com /2011/08/apple-liberal-arts/.
2. Adam Harris, "The liberal arts may not survive the 21st century." *Atlantic,* December 13, 2018.
3. Larry Buchanan, Quoctrung Bul, and Jugal K. Patel, "Black Lives Matter may be the largest movement in U.S. history." *New York Times,* July 3, 2020.
4. "Coronavirus in the U.S.: Latest map and case count." nytimes .com, July 31, 2020. https://www.nytimes.com/interactive /2020/us/coronavirus-us-cases.html.
5. "COVID-19 in racial and ethnic minority groups." cdc.org, June 25, 2020. https://www.cdc.gov/coronavirus/2019-ncov /need-extra-precautions/racial-ethnic-minorities.html.
6. Hollie Silverman et al., "Navajo Nation surpasses New York state for the highest Covid-19 infection rate in the US." CNN, May 18, 2020. https://www.cnn.com/2020/05/18/us/navajo -nation-infection-rate-trnd/index.html.
7. Stacy Weiner, "The new coronavirus affects us all. But some groups may suffer more." aamc.org, March 18, 2020. https:// www.aamc.org/news-insights/new-coronavirus-affects-us-all -some-groups-may-suffer-more.

8. Anna North, "The shift to online learning could worsen educational inequality." vox.com, April 9, 2020. https://www .vox.com/2020/4/9/21200159/coronavirus-school-digital-low -income-students-covid-new-york.

9. Stop AAPI Hate Report: "800+ reported incidents of anti-AAPI hate in California since COVID." June 30, 2020. http:// www.asianpacificpolicyandplanningcouncil.org/wp-content /uploads/CA_Report_6_30_20.pdf.

10. Frances M. Beal, *Black Women's Manifesto; Double Jeopardy: To Be Black and Female* (New York: Third World Women's Alliance, 1969).

11. "Mapping Black Lives Matter protests around the world." WBUR.org, June 22, 2020. https://www.wbur.org/hereandnow /2020/06/22/mapping-black-lives-matter-protests.

12. Jaclyn Reiss, "'Get your knee off our necks!' Watch the Al Sharpton speech that got multiple standing ovations at George Floyd's memorial." bostonglobe.com, June 4, 2020. https:// www.bostonglobe.com/2020/06/04/nation/get-your-knee -off-our-necks-listen-al-sharpton-speech-that-got-multiple -standing-ovations-george-floyds-memorial/.

13. "Lynching in America: Confronting the legacy of racial terror." eji.org. https://lynchinginamerica.eji.org/.

14. Harry Bushnell, "How a 'rogue' employee forced NFL, Goodell into new Black Lives Matter stance." sports.yahoo.com, June 6, 2020. https://sports.yahoo.com/nfl-video-roger-goodell-racism -black-lives-matter-players-employees-110927703.html.

15. "Bubba Wallace praises NASCAR'S Confederate flag ban but one driver says he's quitting over decision." cbsnews.com, June 11, 2020. https://www.cbsnews.com/news/bubba-wallace -driver-nascar-confederate-flag-ban-black-lives-matter/.

16. Greg Bensinger, "Corporate America says Black lives matter. It needs to hold up a mirror." *New York Times,* June 15, 2020.

17. Jemima McEvoy, "Here are all the brands that are changing racist names and packaging." forbes.com, June 26, 2020. https://www.forbes.com/sites/jemimamcevoy/2020/06/25

/here-are-all-the-brands-that-are-changing-racist-names-and
-packaging/#7916afcb37d2.

18. "President Eisgruber's message to community on removal of
Woodrow Wilson name from public policy school and Wilson
College." princeton.edu, June 27, 2020. https://www.princeton
.edu/news/2020/06/27/president-eisgrubers-message
-community-removal-woodrow-wilson-name-public-policy.

19. "Remarks by President Trump at South Dakota's 2020
Mount Rushmore fireworks celebration, Keystone, South
Dakota." Issued July 4, 2020. https://www.whitehouse.gov
/briefings-statements/remarks-president-trump-south
-dakotas-2020-mount-rushmore-fireworks-celebration
-keystone-south-dakota/.

20. Martin Luther King Jr., "Sermon." Delivered March 8, 1965,
in Selma, Alabama. The full text of the section captured by
this paraphrase can be found at https://www.snopes.com/fact
-check/mlk-our-lives-begin-to-end/.

1. RACE AND RACISM IN AMERICAN PUBLIC LIFE

1. The 1619 Project. https://www.nytimes.com/interactive/2019
/08/14/magazine/1619-america-slavery.html.

2. Jake Silverstein, "Why we published the 1619 Project." December 20, 2019. https://www.nytimes.com/interactive/2019/12/20
/magazine/1619-intro.html.

3. Steve Luxenberg, "The Jim Crow car: The North, the South
and the forgotten origins of racial separation." *Washington Post
Magazine*, February 24, 2019.

4. "African Americans." stateofworkingamerica.org. http://
stateofworkingamerica.org/fact-sheets/african-americans/.

5. Heather Boushey and Somin Park, "Fighting inequality is key
to preparing for the next recession." Economic Policy Institute:
Working Economics Blog, May 15, 2019. https://www.epi.org

/blog/fighting-inequality-is-key-to-preparing-for-the-next
-recession/.

6. Kimberlé Crenshaw, "Demarginalizing the intersection of race
   and sex: A Black feminist critique of antidiscrimination doctrine, feminist theory and antiracist politics," *The University
   of Chicago Legal Forum,* 1989, 139–67. http://chicagounbound
   .uchicago.edu/uclf/vol1989/iss1/8.

7. Beverly Guy-Sheftall and Johnnetta Betsch Cole, eds., *Words of
   Fire: An Anthology of African-American Feminist Thought* (New
   York: New Press, 1995), 289.

8. Josh Gabbatiss, "James Watson: The most controversial
   statements made by the father of DNA." independent.co.uk,
   January 13, 2019. http://www.independent.co.uk/news/science
   /james-watson-racism-sexism-dna-race-intelligence-genetics
   -double-helix-a8725556.html.

9. Richard A. Goldsby and Mary Catherine Bateson, *Thinking
   Race: Social Myths and Biological Realities* (Lanham, Maryland:
   Rowman and Littlefield, 2019).

10. "The biggest lie in the White supremacist propaganda play-
    book: Unraveling the truth about 'Black-on-White' crime."
    June 14, 2018. https://www.splcenter.org/20180614/biggest-lie
    -white-supremacist-propaganda-playbook-unraveling-truth
    -about-'black-white-crime.

11. "Segregation in America," 2018, 10. https://
    segregationinamerica.eji.org/report.pdf.

12. Ida B. Wells, "On lynch law in America." Speech given January
    1900 in Chicago. https://etc.usf.edu/lit2go/185/civil-rights
    -and-conflict-in-the-united-states-selected-speeches/4375
    /speech-on-lynch-law-in-america-given-by-ida-b-wells-in
    -chicago-illinois-january-1900/.

13. Erin Blakemore, "The brutal history of anti-Latino dis-
    crimination in America." history.com, September 27, 2017.
    www.history.com/news/the-brutal-history-of-anti-latino
    -discrimination-in-america.

2. THE NEED FOR COURAGEOUS CONVERSATIONS ABOUT RACE AND RACISM IN AMERICAN PUBLIC LIFE

1. Howard J. Ross, *Our Search for Belonging: How Our Need to Connect Is Tearing Us Apart* (San Francisco: Berrett-Koehler, 2018).
2. John Hope Franklin, *From Slavery to Freedom,* 8th edition (New York: McGraw-Hill, 2000), 243.
3. W. E. B. Du Bois, "Black Reconstruction in America: An Essay toward a History of the Part which Black Folk Played in the Attempt to Reconstruct Democracy in America, 1860–1880" (New York: Harcourt, Brace, 1935).
4. W. E. B. Du Bois, *The Souls of Black Folk,* with an introduction by Henry Louis Gates Jr. (New York: Bantam Books, 1989 edition), 5.
5. James Allen, ed., *Without Sanctuary: Lynching Photography in America* (Santa Fe, New Mexico: Twin Palms, 2000).
6. Jacey Fortin, "Congress moves to make lynching a federal crime after 120 years of failure." *New York Times,* February 26, 2020.
7. Michelle Alexander, *The New Jim Crow: Mass Incarceration in the Age of Colorblindness* (New York: New Press, 2010).
8. "The Legacy Museum: From enslavement to mass incarceration." https://museumandmemorial.eji.org/.
9. "Criminal justice fact sheet." naacp.org. https://www.naacp.org/criminal-justice-fact-sheet/.
10. "Quick facts: United States," census.gov. https://www.census.gov/quickfacts/fact/table/US/PST045218.
11. "Criminal justice fact sheet," naacp.org. https://www.naacp.org/criminal-justice-fact-sheet/.
12. Khalil Gibran Muhammad, *The Condemnation of Blackness: Race, Crime, and the Making of Modern Urban America* (Cambridge, Massachusetts: Harvard University Press, 2010), 1.
13. Muhammad, *The Condemnation of Blackness,* 1.

14. Ida B. Wells-Barnett, *The Light of Truth: Writings of an Anti-Lynching Crusader* (New York: Penguin, 2014).

15. Paula Giddings, *Ida: A Sword Among Lions: Ida B. Wells and the Campaign Against Lynching* (New York, Harper Collins, 2009).

16. Ta-Nehisi Coates, "The case for reparations," *Atlantic,* June 2014.

17. Since 1952, Germany has granted $89 billion in reparations on behalf of Jewish survivors of the Holocaust.

18. David Brooks, "The case for reparations." *New York Times,* March 7, 2019.

19. Gabrielle Bruney, "David Brooks' support of reparations gets one thing incredibly wrong." esquire.com, March 8, 2019. https://www.esquire.com/news-politics/a26765432/david-brooks-reparations/.

20. Nikole Hannah-Jones, "The end of the postracial myth." *New York Times,* November 15, 2016.

21. "Segregation in America," 2018. https://segregationinamerica.eji.org/report/how-segregation-survived.html.

22. Torrance G. Latham, "Our new civil rights movement will begin in our schools." In *The Burden: African Americans and the Enduring Impact of Slavery,* ed. Rochelle Riley et al. (Detroit: Wayne State University Press, 2018), 141–44.

3. IMAGINE OUR NATION WITHOUT RACISM

1. Debbie Lord, "What happened at Charlottesville: Looking back on the rally that ended in death." ajc.com, August 13, 2019. https://www.ajc.com/news/national/what-happened-charlottesville-looking-back-the-anniversary-the-deadly-rally/fPpnLrbAtbxSwNI9BEy93K/amp.html.

2. Brett Murphy, "Blackface, KKK hoods and mock lynchings: Review of 900 yearbooks finds blatant racism." *USA Today,* February 21, 2019. https://www.usatoday.com/in-depth/news/investigations/2019/02/20/blackface-racist-photos-yearbooks

-colleges-kkk-lynching-mockery-fraternities-black-70-s-80-s
/2858921002/.

3. Cleve R. Wootson Jr., "A black Yale student fell asleep in her dorm's common room. A white student called police." *Washington Post,* May 11, 2018.

4. Craig Steven Wilder, *Ebony and Ivy: Race, Slavery, and the Troubled History of America's Universities* (New York: Bloomsbury, 2013), 1–2.

5. Ibid, 11.

6. Carter G. Woodson, *The Mis-Education of the Negro* (n.p.: Feather Trail Press, 2009,) chapter 18.

7. "Key events in Black higher education." jbhe.com. https://www .jbhe.com/chronology/.

8. Ibid. For information on segregation in Washington, D.C., see Tikia K. Hamilton, "The cost of integration: The contentious career of Garnet C. Wilkinson." *Washington History,* Spring 2018. See also her forthcoming book, *Making a Model System: Battle for Educational Equality in the Nation's Capital before Brown.*

9. Linda M. Perkins, "The racial integration of the Seven Sister colleges." *Journal of Blacks in Higher Education,* 19, Spring 1998, 104–8.

10. Roslyn Clark Artis, "How we must fix the worst Black History Month ever." hbcudigest.com, February 28, 2019. https:// hbcudigest.com/how-we-must-fix-the-worst-black-history -month-ever/.

11. "Fast facts: Historically Black colleges and universities." nces .ed.gov. https://nces.ed.gov/fastfacts/display.asp?id=667.

12. Ibid.

13. Artis, "How we must fix the worst Black History Month ever."

14. Crystal R. Sanders, "Katherine Johnson should also be remembered for desegregating higher education." *Washington Post,* February 25, 2020.

15. Martha Biondi, *The Black Revolution on Campus* (Oakland: University of California Press, 2014), 2.

16. Sonam Sheth, "Trump equates Confederate generals Robert E. Lee and Stonewall Jackson with George Washington in bizarre press conference." businessinsider.com, August 15, 2017. https://www.businessinder.com/trump-robert-e-lee-stonewall-jackson-george-washington-thomas-jefferson-2017-18.

17. I. Wright, "Fight the power: Can protestors ever ask for too much?" hellobeautiful.com, December 4, 2015. https://hellobeautiful.com/2830598/princeton-university-protests-2/.

18. "Fast facts: Race/ethnicity of college faculty." https://nces.ed.gov/fastfacts/display.asp?id=61.

19. Jennifer Ma, Matea Pender, and Meredith Welch, "Education pays: The benefits of higher education for individuals and society." Trends in Higher Education Series, College Board, 2019, 4, 8, 15. https://research.collegeboard.org/pdf/education-pays-2019-full-report.pdf; Emily Tate, "College rates and race." insidehighered.com, April 26, 2017. https://www.insidehighered.com/news/2017/04/26/college-completion-rates-vary-race-and-ethnicity-report-finds.

20. Anthony Abraham Jack, *The Privileged Poor: How Elite Colleges Are Failing Disadvantaged Students* (Cambridge, Massachusetts: Harvard University Press, 2019).

21. Reshmi Dutt-Ballerstadt, "Academic prioritization or killing the liberal arts?" *Inside Higher Ed,* March 1, 2019.

22. Rudolph P. Byrd, Johnnetta Betsch Cole, and Beverly Guy-Sheftall, eds., *I Am Your Sister: Collected and Unpublished Writings of Audre Lorde* (Oxford, United Kingdom: Oxford University Press, 2010).

23. Frederick Douglass, "Address on West India emancipation." Delivered August 4, 1857.

AFTERWORD

1. For further study, please see Kabria Baumgartner, *In Pursuit of Knowledge: Black Women and Educational Activism in Antebellum America* (New York: New York University Press, 2019).

2. Anna Julia Cooper, *A Voice from the South,* with an introduction by Mary Helen Washington (New York: Oxford University Press, 1988, originally published 1892), 144.

3. Heather Andrea Williams, *Self-Taught: African American Education in Slavery and Freedom* (Chapel Hill: University of North Carolina Press, 2005), 7.

4. Russell J. Rickford, *We Are an African People: Independent Education, Black Power, and the Radical Imagination* (Oxford, United Kingdom: Oxford University Press, 2016).

5. See Ibram X. Kendi, *Stamped from the Beginning: The Definitive History of Racist Ideas in America* (New York: Bold Type Books, 2016).

6. W. E. B. Du Bois, *The Souls of Black Folk,* with an introduction by Henry Louis Gates Jr. (New York: Bantam Books, 1989 edition), 7.

7. Alberto Alesina, Edward Glaeser, and Bruce Sacerdote, "Why doesn't the U.S. have a European-style welfare state." scholar.harvard.edu, November 2001. https://scholar.harvard.edu/files/glaeser/files/why_doesnt_the_u.s._have_a_european-style_welfare_state.pdf. For earlier history see Daniel T. Rodgers, *Atlantic Crossings: Social Politics in a Progressive Age* (Cambridge, Massachusetts: Belknap Press of Harvard University Press, 1998).

8. Marcia Chatelain, *Franchise: The Golden Arches in Black America* (New York: Liveright, 2020).

9. Maya Salam, "For Serena Williams, childbirth was a harrowing ordeal. She's not alone." *New York Times,* January 11, 2018.

10. Deirdre Cooper Owens, *Medical Bondage: Race, Gender, and the Origins of American Gynecology* (Athens: University of Georgia Press, 2017).

11. https://healthinherhue.com/about; Janelle Okwodu, "Serena Williams on the message behind her new campaign and staying grounded during isolation." vogue.com, May 8, 2020. https://www.vogue.com/article/serena-williams-stuart-weitzman-campaign-vital-voices-interview.

12. "COVID-19 Coronavirus pandemic." https://www
.worldometers.info/coronavirus/.

13. Meagan Flynn, "'Those numbers take your breath away':
COVID-19 is hitting Chicago's Black neighborhoods much
harder than others, officials say." *Washington Post,* April 7,
2020.

14. Anya Kamenetz, "4 in 10 U.S. teens say they haven't done
online learning since schools closed." npr.org, April 8, 2020.
https://www.npr.org/sections/coronavirus-live-updates/2020
/04/08/829618124/4-in-10-u-s-teens-say-they-havent-done
-online-learning-since-schools-closed?utm_medium=social&
utm_campaign=npr&utm_source=facebook.com&utm_term=
nprnews&fbclid=IwAR2CKLHTBDqWDV5QIGDaPcHyVtU-
aipiCLqz4MPVdWFCRT6-tPcKVCxo47EI.

15. See E. Franklin Frazier, *Black Bourgeoisie* (New York: Free
Press, 1957).

16. Anna Julia Cooper, *A Voice from the South,* 29.

17. Stacey Abrams, "Commentary: My $200,000 debt should not
disqualify me for governor of Georgia." fortune.com, April 24,
2018. https://fortune.com/2018/04/24/stacey-abrams-debt
-georgia-governor/.

18. Judith Scott-Clayton and Jing Li, "Black-White disparity
in student loan debt more than triples after graduation."
brookings.edu, October 20, 2016. https://www.brookings.edu
/research/black-white-disparity-in-student-loan-debt-more
-than-triples-after-graduation/.

19. Carter G. Woodson, *The Mis-Education of the Negro* (n.p.:
Feather Trail Press, 2009), 28.

20. Interview with Bianca Baldridge, author of *Reclaiming Community: Race and the Uncertain Future of Youth Work* (Stanford,
California: Stanford University Press, 2019).

21. "Why U.S. needs Black Lives Matter movement today." npr.org,
May 29, 2020. https://www.npr.org/2020/05/29/865685777
/why-u-s-needs-black-lives-matter-movement-today.

22. Stephanie E. Jones-Rogers, *They Were Her Property: White
Women as Slave Owners in the American South* (New Haven:

Yale University Press, 2019); Tikia K. Hamilton, "'Votes for Women': Race, Gender, and Individualism in the Age of Jim Crow" (forthcoming journal article, 2021).

23. Tikia K. Hamilton, "America's private, White, elite schools need reform. Now." momentum.medium.com, June 26, 2020. https://medium.com/@tikiakhamilton/the-death-of-diversity -a-call-for-radical-reform-in-pwis-3a5018065aa.

24. I. Wright, "Fight the power: Can protestors ever ask for too much?" hellobeautiful.com, December 4, 2015. https:// hellobeautiful.com/2830598/princeton-university-protests-2/.

25. Kellie Carter Jackson, "The double standard of the American riot." theatlantic.com, June 1, 2020. https://www.theatlantic .com/culture/archive/2020/06/riots-are-american-way-george -floyd-protests/612466/. See also Kellie Carter Jackson, *Force and Freedom: Black Abolitionists and the Politics of Violence* (Philadelphia: University of Pennsylvania Press, 2019).

26. See Brittney C. Cooper, *Beyond Respectability: The Intellectual Thought of Race Women* (Urbana: University of Illinois Press, 2017).

27. Anna Julia Cooper, *A Voice from the South,* 47.

THE MALCOLM LESTER PHI BETA KAPPA LECTURES ON LIBERAL ARTS AND PUBLIC LIFE

The Problem with Rules: Essays on the Meaning and
Value of Liberal Education
JOHN CHURCHILL